D0421943

Prop. of Jane proay

THE SNOW BALL ***

THE SNOW BALL

THE SNOW BALL ***

A.R. Gurney

Garden City, New York

© Copyright 1992, by A.R. Gurney

CAUTION: Professionals and amateurs are hereby warned that THE SNOW BALL is subject to a royalty. It is fully protected under the copyright laws of the United States of America, and of all countries covered by the International Copyright Union (including the Dominion of Canada and the rest of the British Commonwealth), and of all countries covered by the Pan-American Copyright Covention and the Universal Copyright Convention, and of all countries with which the United States has reciprocal copyright relations. All rights, including professional, amateur, motion picture, recitation, lecturing, public reading, radio broadcasting, television, video or sound taping, all other forms of mechanical or electronic reproduction, such as information storage and retrieval systems and photocopying, and the rights of translation into foreign languages, are strictly reserved. Particular emphasis is laid upon the question of readings, permission for which must be secured from the author's agent in writing.

The stock and amateur production rights in THE SNOW BALL are controlled exclusively by the DRAMATISTS PLAY SERVICE, INC., 440 Park Avenue South, New York, N.Y. 10016. No stock or amateur performance of the play may be given without obtaining in advance the written permission of the DRAMATISTS PLAY SERVICE, INC., and paying the requisite fee.

All inquiries concerning rights (other than stock and amateur rights) should be addressed to William Morris Agency, Inc., 1350 Avenue of the Americas, New York, N.Y. 10019, Attention: Gilbert Parker

ISBN: 1-56865-074-4

Photographs of the 1992 Old Globe Theatre production San Diego, CA by Ken Howard
Design by Maria Chiarino
Manufactured in the United States of America

To Jack O'Brien
and
Graciela Daniele

THE SNOW BALL was produced at the Hartford Stage Company (Mark Lamos, Artistic Director; David Haukanson, Managing Director), in Hartford, Connecticut, on February 9, 1991. It was directed by Jack O'Brien; the set design was by Douglas W. Schmidt; the costume design was by Steven Rubin; the lighting design was by David F. Segal; the sound design was by Jeff Ladman; the choreographer was Graciela Daniele; the ballroom coach was Willie Rosario and the production stage manager was Barbara Reo. The cast was as follows:

COOPER JONES . . . . James R. Winker
LUCY DUNBAR . . . . Kandis Chappell
LIZ JONES . . . . Katherine McGrath
VAN DAM, BALDWIN HALL . . . . Tom Lacy
YOUNG JACK . . . . Christopher Wells
YOUNG KITTY . . . . Susan J. Coon
SAUL RADNER . . . . Robert Phalen
JOAN DALEY . . . . Deborah Taylor
JACK DALEY . . . . Donald Wayne
KITTY PRICE . . . . Rita Gardner
VARIOUS MEMBERS OF THE COMMUNITY
AS CHILDREN AND ADULTS . . . . . . Mary R. Barnett,
Terrence Caza, Brian John Driscoll, Cynthia D. Hanson, Robert Phalen, Mimi Quillin, Deborah Taylor, John Thomas Waite

THE SNOW BALL was subsequently produced at the Old Globe Theatre in San Diego, California, on May 4, 1991, and at the Huntington Theatre in Boston, Massachusetts, on September 25, 1991, with much of the same cast. In these two productions, Douglas Pagliotti was the production stage manager. In Boston, George Deloy and Deborah May played COOPER and LUCY.

CHARACTERS

(sixteen actors, minimum)

Individual parts:

COOPER JONES

LIZ, his wife

LUCY DUNBAR, his friend

JACK DALEY, as a young man

JACK DALEY, as an older man

KITTY PRICE, as a young woman

KITTY PRICE, as an older woman

Multiple parts:

MR. VAN DAM and BALDWIN HALL

SAUL RADNER, WORKMAN and FRITZI KLINGER

JOAN DALEY, BARBARA FISKE and RHODA RADNER

GINNY WATERS and TELEVISION INTERVIEWER

BILLY WICKWIRE, TELEVISION CAMERAMAN and
   WAITER

CALVIN POTTER, MUSICIAN and WAITER

HEATHER HEALY and WAITRESS

BREWSTER DUNN, MR. SMITHERS and WORKMAN

MARY MONTESANO and OTHERS

SETTING

The play takes place primarily in the Cotillion Room, an elegant ballroom in the old George Washington Hotel, in a large mid-western city. There is a sumptuous staircase, a good dance floor, surrounded by small tables and gilt bent-wood chairs, and a high palladian window looking out at a downtown skyline. Snow may be seen through the window as necessary. A rolling table, serving as a blue print stand at the beginning, may become a desk, a bar, a counter and so forth.

The play is designed to be performed to recorded music.

The time is today and yesterday.

ACT ONE ✳✳✳

At rise: A spotlight isolates a young couple, JACK DALEY *and* KITTY PRICE, *dancing elegantly, spinning, turning, dipping, with a wonderful casual ease to the sounds of a lovely old tune played by a brisk society band. Behind them, through the window, we can see large snowflakes slowly drifting down.*

COOPER JONES, *a middle-aged man in a raincoat, enters down the staircase, watches them and then speaks to the audience.*

COOPER: Jack Daley and Kitty Price were the best dancers in town. There is absolutely no doubt about that. It took your breath away to watch them. A kind of special space would emerge around them on the dance floor, as the rest of us would step back to give them room, and then stand around and watch them dance. (*He watches them for a moment*) Of course, they weren't quite so good when they were dancing with someone else. (BILLY WICKWIRE *cuts in on* KITTY) Kitty would be light on her feet, and follow fairly well, but she'd always get a little lazy, and run into trouble on the turns . . . (*We see this.* HEATHER HEALY *comes on to dance with* JACK) And the girls used to say, when they danced with Jack, that he was always looking over their shoulders, looking for Kitty, yearning for a time to dance with her again . . . (*We see this, too. Then they change partners so that* JACK *is once again dancing with* KITTY. *The other couple disappears*) But together Jack and Kitty were unbeatable. For a few years there, in the center of the century, they ruled the roost. They were by far the best at dancing school, the main attraction at all the other parties and topped even themselves at the Snow Ball . . . (*The light fades on the dancers. The music fades into the sound of hammering and power tools, as the lights come up on the Cotillion Room. We see a lad-*

der, a worktable with blueprints, as two workmen finish up for the day. Through the window, we see the lights from other downtown buildings, glassy and modern. It is late afternoon, late fall. LUCY DUNBAR, *also middle-aged, also in an overcoat, hurries in*)

LUCY (*breathlessly*): Sorry I'm late. Our sweet little bookstore has just been bought out by what is called "a chain." Which means they chain us to the checkout counters. I had to plead temporary insanity to get away.

COOPER: I've been looking around.

LUCY: I knew you would. . . . Doesn't it ring a wonderful old bell?

COOPER: A bell, at least.

LUCY: Dancing school?

COOPER: Jack and Kitty . . .

LUCY: The Snow Ball?

COOPER: Jack and Kitty dancing at the Snow Ball . . . (*A glimpse of* JACK *and* KITTY, *dancing in the shadows*)

LUCY: We're making the room exactly the way it was, Cooper. Floor, furniture, everything. We had it legally landmarked.

COOPER: I can see.

LUCY: The rest of this hotel, the rest of downtown, the rest of the *world* can be redeveloped to *death* for all I care, but this room stays exactly the same.

COOPER: Good work.

LUCY: I thought you, of all people, should see.

COOPER: What's that supposed to mean?

LUCY: Well, I mean, you sold the building.

COOPER: The bank sold it.

LUCY: You made the *deal*, Cooper. You were the real estate broker for the whole operation.

COOPER: It's what I do, Lucy.

LUCY: Oh yes. And you did it. I just hope you made a huge pile of money.

COOPER: I made almost enough to keep two kids in college another term.

LUCY: Well, the point is, a few of us managed to save this room.

COOPER: I'm glad you did. (*A workman passes by, putting on his coat*)

WORKMAN: 'Night, Mrs. Dunbar.

LUCY: Goodnight, Eddie.

ANOTHER WORKMAN (*indicating the window*): Starting to snow. (*They leave*)

LUCY (*calling after them*): Drive carefully! (*Pause. They look at each other*)

COOPER: I'd better get home, too. (*Starts out*)

LUCY: I'm thinking of bringing it back, Cooper.

COOPER: Bringing what back?

LUCY: The Snow Ball. This Christmas. To reopen this room.

COOPER: Oh come on . . .

LUCY: And I want you to help me organize it.

COOPER: Why me?

LUCY: I need your clout. You're a civic leader around here.

COOPER: Not these days, Lucy.

LUCY: You ran the Symphony Drive. You did that work for the zoo . . .

COOPER: I don't do dances.

LUCY: You owe it to me, Cooper.

COOPER: *Owe* it to you?

LUCY: And to yourself.

COOPER: Oh please.

LUCY: You sold your heritage!

COOPER: Oh for Chrissake!

LUCY: Your grandfather *built* this building! Your father kept it going. And you let the whole thing slip through your fingers!

COOPER: Times change!

LUCY: If we let them.

COOPER: Life goes on, Lucy.

LUCY: Life? Is that life out there? In those great, glass buildings? Or in that lonely walk-up I go home to these days? Is that *life?* Or was this life, right here, in this lovely old room?

COOPER: *Was* is the operative word.

LUCY: And could be again. At least for one night.

COOPER: It would never work without Jack and Kitty. (JACK *and* KITTY *glide through the shadows*)

LUCY: Then we'll bring them back, too!

COOPER: You're a hopeless romantic, Lucy.

LUCY (*touching his arm*): Me? What about you? I *know* you, Cooper Jones. I used to dance with you, remember? (*He goes to look out the window*)

COOPER: It's early for snow.

LUCY: See? It's a good omen.

COOPER: Or a warning.

LUCY: Oh please, Cooper. Let's do it. Let's put our best foot forward, one last time.

COOPER: Better get home.

LUCY: And I've got to get back to the chain gang. We're doing inventory, God help us. Everything over six months old gets immediately remaindered. Even the Bible will be fifty percent off. (*Starts out*)

COOPER: Need a ride?

LUCY: No thanks. Gordon at least left me a car. . . . Will you do it, Cooper?

COOPER: Liz would laugh in my face.

LUCY: Well, if she won't dance with you, I will . . .

COOPER: I haven't danced in twenty years.

LUCY: It'll all come back, I promise . . . (*She hurries off. The lights focus in on* COOPER. *Behind, in a dim light, the Cotillion Room begins to emerge as it once looked. Off to one side, a group of boys gathers in the shadows. They wear white shirts and dark blue suits and shined shoes*)

BREWSTER DANN (*calling to* COOPER): Come on, Cooper! You can't get out of it!

BILLY WICKWIRE: No one gets out of dancing school!

FRITZI KLINGER: Unless you get the mumps.

BREWSTER (*clutching his groin*): Aaagh! Which is almost worth it. (*On the other side, a group of girls begins to gather, all in formal dresses with white gloves and black patent leather shoes. They primp and giggle*)

BARBARA FISKE: Is it true you hate girls, Cooper?

GINNY WATERS: Or are you just shy?

HEATHER HEALY: He's cute when he blushes.

LIZ (*as a young girl*): Boys never know what to say.

BARBARA: That's why they have to go to dancing school.

COOPER (*becoming a boy*): I'll never go to dancing school. Ever. If they send me, I'll walk right out and go to the movies.

BREWSTER: Five bucks says you don't.

COOPER: Shake. (*They shake hands. The handshake turns into Indian wrestling, which degenerates into a chaotic wrestling match on the floor, as the boys cheer and the girls squeal and shriek.* MR. VAN DAM, *the dancing master, a portly man in tails, appears from the shadows. He taps his walking stick on the floor for order. The boys quickly break up their fight, and scamper to their seats on one side of the room. The girls hurry to the other.* COOPER *gets caught in the center without a chair, has to find one. When things are settled,* VAN DAM *slowly parades in front of the class, inspecting it.* LUCY, *now in a formal dress, has by now joined the girls*)

VAN DAM: Posture! Posture! Show the world a straight back! (*He moves up the line*) I am looking at feet, I am looking at hands, I am looking at fingernails.

BREWSTER (*to himself*): Oh Christ. I forgot to pee.

BARBARA (*to herself*): I'm getting a pimple on my nose. It feels like Mount Monadnock!

VAN DAM: The young ladies, while seated, will keep their heels, and knees, together, with their hands folded delicately, palms upward, in their laps. (*The girls do this*)

FRITZI (*to himself*): What a waste of time! I could be organizing my comic books.

LIZ (*to herself*): I hate being new at places. Everybody knows everybody, and nobody knows me.

VAN DAM: The young gentlemen, on the other hand, will keep their legs somewhat apart, with each hand resting lightly on each knee, palms downward, in a manly fashion. (*The boys do this. They begin to communicate with each other*)

CALVIN (*to his neighbor*): I wanted to bring my dog, but my parents wouldn't let me.

BREWSTER (*indicating the row of girls*): There's plenty of dogs right here. (*VAN DAM is now taking a furtive slug from a silver flask*)

HEATHER (*whispering to her neighbor*): Do you realize we're missing the entire *Hit Parade?*

MARY: My little brother's making a list of the songs.

BILLY (*to* COOPER): Why do we have to come here, anyway?

COOPER: My mother says it will make us better husbands.

FRITZI: My father says it will make us better lovers. (*The others look at him; he shrugs*)

LUCY (*to another girl*): I just read *Peyton Place.*

MARY: I hear that's a dirty book.

LUCY: Oh it is! They even take a shower together.

LIZ (*to* BARBARA): My name's Liz. My mother sent me here to make friends.

BARBARA: I have too many friends. But I could squeeze you in on Saturday mornings.

COOPER (*to* BREWSTER): This afternoon, we saw Rita Hayworth in *Gilda.*

BREWSTER: Boiingg! (VAN DAM *notices* BILLY)

VAN DAM: Mr. Wickwire, we do not wear white socks to dancing school.

BILLY: I was playing hockey, sir. I hardly had time to change my pants. (*Giggles from all*)

VAN DAM: Gentlemen bathe, Mr. Wickwire. Gentlemen change their stockings and their linen. And gentlemen say "trousers" instead of "pants."

BILLY: Yes sir.

VAN DAM: Mr. Cromeier, may I review the music? (*He exits*)

BARBARA: I hate boys. I hate their guts.

HEATHER: I wish they weren't so basically grubby.

MARY: You're cheating, Lucy. You're wearing a bra!

LUCY: This is just Kleenex. It doesn't count.

BREWSTER: Who farted? Somebody cut the cheese around here. (VAN DAM *comes back, tapping his stick*)

VAN DAM: The young gentlemen will now ask the young ladies to dance. (*The boys reluctantly cross the floor, jockeying for position.* LIZ *goes up to* VAN DAM. *Whispers in his ear*) What?

. . . Again? . . . Oh go on. (LIZ *scurries out*) The young gentlemen will bow. (*The boys bow awkwardly*) The young ladies will rise and curtsy. (*The girls do*) Handkerchiefs out. . . . Positions, please. . . . One, two, three . . . (*The boys take handkerchiefs out of their pockets and put them in their right hands, so as not to soil the girls' dresses*) One, two, three, four . . . (*They assume the dancing position.* VAN DAM *taps his stick again*) We will now review the schottische. . . . Music, Mr. Cromeier, if you please. (*The music begins: some simple two-step, played very slowly. The couples move stiffly, as* VAN DAM, *with his stick, moves among them*) Small steps, please. . . . And one and two and. . . . Gently, please. . . . If you young ladies and gentlemen can't learn the simple schottische, how do you ever expect to dance at the Snow Ball?

LUCY (*to* COOPER, *as they dance*): Isn't this fun?

COOPER (*sullenly*): Oh yeah. Sure. Goodie goodie gumdrop.

LUCY: No, but just think. Last week, you chased me home from school. And now you're *dancing* with me.

COOPER: I plan to get out, you know. Errol Flynn got out of Nazi Germany, and so will I.

LUCY: But why? Dancing can be a wonderful way of getting to know people.

COOPER: Stop talking, please. I'm planning my escape.

(*They dance.* LIZ, *now in modern clothes, stands at a table. She combs her hair in "a mirror." The music continues under*)

LIZ (*calling to* COOPER *as he dances*): What's this I hear about reviving the Snow Ball?

COOPER (*coming out of the dance*): What? There's talk of it. Yes. (*The dancers dance off*)

LIZ: From Lucy Dunbar, I'll bet.

COOPER (*going through the mail on the table*): Lucy is exploring the idea, yes.

LIZ: Ever since her divorce, she's had a bug up her ass.

COOPER: Jesus, Liz.

LIZ: Well she has. And I didn't like that kiss she gave you the other night.

COOPER: She was wishing me a happy birthday.

LIZ: Oh is that what she was wishing?

COOPER: She's recovering from a rough marriage, Liz. They say that guy used to beat her up.

LIZ: And how does the Snow Ball solve that?

COOPER: I imagine she wants to be treated like a lady again.

LIZ: I imagine she wants to meet another man. (*She gets her bag*)

COOPER: Where're you going?

LIZ: I've got a meeting. Down at the office.

COOPER: At seven in the evening?

LIZ: It's the only time we could all meet. There's that macaroni stuff in the freezer.

COOPER: Sounds delicious. (*Reads his mail*) What's this "Lab supplies" for Teddy? I thought he hated science.

LIZ: That's a film course. It's called "Film Lab." They make films.

COOPER: 235 bucks! What's he making? *Ten Commandments Two?*

LIZ: Now now.

COOPER: No science, no foreign language, no history. Next term he at least has to take a history course. Agreed?

LIZ: Agreed.

COOPER: He who ignores the past is doomed to repeat it.

LIZ: I said I agreed. (*Pause*)

COOPER: But you don't like the idea of the Snow Ball.

LIZ: I think it sucks.

COOPER: Liz, hey, your language. You've been working with street people too long.

LIZ (*putting on lipstick*): Well at least I'm not Lucy Dunbar, digging up dead dogs.

COOPER: She got them to refurbish the Cotillion Room. That's a good thing.

LIZ: I guess.

COOPER: You *guess?* We met in that room. We had our wedding reception there.

LIZ: It was a lovely room . . .

COOPER: Why not reopen it with a splash?

LIZ: Because no one *dances* that way any more, Cooper. Kids don't know how to, and grown-ups don't want to.

COOPER: I want to.

LIZ: Oh come on.

COOPER (*trying to dance with her*): I remember a time when you wanted to.

LIZ (*breaking away*): Cooper, I am late. It's a meeting on homelessness, and I happen to be running it.

COOPER (*watching her get ready*): There's even talk of bringing back Jack and Kitty. (*Young* JACK *and* KITTY *are seen dancing*)

LIZ: Jack and Kitty haven't even *seen* each other in several centuries.

COOPER: Still. There's talk.

LIZ: Don't tell me you're personally involved in all this.

COOPER: I'm thinking about it.

LIZ: Oh Lord, Cooper. You always go overboard on these things. First it was the Philharmonic. Then the zoo . . .

COOPER: I happen to care about endangered species.

LIZ: Well I'm sorry, but I can't get wound up over some dumb dance while this city disintegrates around us.

COOPER: Maybe you'd like to turn the Cotillion Room into a shelter.

LIZ: Better that than having a bunch of old Wasps waddle around the dance floor!

COOPER: Don't knock your roots all the time, Liz!

LIZ: The hell with roots! Roots hold you down!

COOPER: They also keep you alive.

LIZ: You can't turn back the clock, Cooper!

COOPER: So I'm left to turn on the microwave.

LIZ: Cooper, it's snowing like mad, and I'm already late! (*She starts out*)

COOPER (*calling after her*): Homelessness begins at home, Liz! (*Picks up telephone, starts to dial*)

LIZ (*returning*): You made me forget my briefcase. . . . Who're you calling?

COOPER: A friend.

LIZ: Oh.

COOPER: An old friend.

LIZ: Oh.

COOPER: Someone who stays home at the end of the day.

LIZ: Oh, Cooper.

COOPER: Why? Do you care?

LIZ (*kissing him*): Sweetheart, I care about being late at the moment! (*Starts out again*) Oh, and if you go to bed before I'm back, don't forget to turn down the furnace! (*She's out*)

COOPER (*calling after her*): It's already down, toots! I'm worried about the pipes freezing! (*He starts to dial, then turns to the audience*) I mean, Jesus, how do you like that woman? Everyone says she's bloomed since the kids left home, and she got this job—"Liz has bloomed," everybody says. O.K. O.K., she's bloomed, she's a flower, she's a goddam gardenia, but what about me? No. Wrong. What about us? When do we talk, when do we make love, when do we EAT, for Chrissake? (*He starts to dial, then turns to the audience again*) She wants to move out of this house, you know. Oh sure. She wants to sell this fine old house and move. Downtown! To some waterfront condo where she can be quote in the thick of things unquote. What about the garden? What about my grandmother's furniture? What about the goddam dog? "Time to move on," Liz says. "Time to grow." Well maybe it's time to remember who we are. (*He picks up the phone again*) My mother says it's roots that count. That's why Liz and I have lasted so long. That's why the kids have turned out so well. Roots, says my mother. Similar backgrounds. Birds of a feather. All that shit. (*Piano music. The ghostly dancers begin to return*) Well, maybe so. Liz and I sure knew the steps for a while. With each other. With the kids. Maybe that's why I'm hung up on this goddam dance. I want to glide through the world with a woman again, at least for one night! (*Into telephone*) Lucy? Hi. . . . It's me. . . . Hey, on this Snow Ball thing, I think it's one hell of a good idea. (*The dancers return, dancing better than before.* VAN DAM *pounds out the beat with his stick*)

VAN DAM: And one and two and one and two and . . . (LIZ *reappears in her formal dress. She sits in a chair on the sidelines, and then calls to* COOPER *furtively*)

LIZ: Pssst. . . . Hey you! . . . Are you Cooper Jones?

COOPER: What's it to you?

LIZ: You're supposed to dance with me.

COOPER: Says who?

LIZ: Says your mother. I'm new in town, and your mother told my mother you'd ask me to dance.

COOPER: News to me. (*Starts to walk away*)

LIZ: Oh come on. It's like going to the dentist. It prevents problems later on. (COOPER *reluctantly goes to* LIZ, *bows in front of her.* LIZ *gets up from her chair, curtsys to him, and then they join the circle of dancers, dancing stiffly around the room*) Thank you.

COOPER (*grumpily*): You're not welcome.

VAN DAM: And one and two, and small steps two, and one and two and . . .

LIZ: I hear this town is going rapidly downhill.

COOPER: Wrong!

LIZ: My father says we've climbed aboard a sinking ship.

COOPER: For your information, we're the thirteenth largest city in the United States. And our zoo is internationally famous.

LIZ: All I know is, there are bad slums. Next summer I'm going to be a junior counselor for slum kids.

COOPER: Goodie for you.

LIZ: Want to help? They need boys.

COOPER: No thanks. I'm going to tennis camp.

LIZ: You're kind of superficial, aren't you?

COOPER: At least I'm not a do-gooder.

LIZ: At least I care about other people.

COOPER: At least I—are you wearing perfume?

LIZ: Sure. Smell. (*She offers her neck*) I swiped it from my mother. (COOPER *furtively sniffs her neck*) Like it?

COOPER: At least you don't have B.O. (*They dance closer.* VAN DAM *notices*)

VAN DAM: Mr. Jones: just what do you think you're doing?

COOPER: Making quiet conversation, sir.

VAN DAM: Come to the center of the circle, please!

COOPER (*to* LIZ; *under his breath*): Thanks a bunch.

LIZ: I didn't do anything.

COOPER: You seduced me.

VAN DAM: We're waiting, Mr. Jones! The rest of you may take your seats. (COOPER *goes to the center. The other boys and girls sit down*) Please demonstrate the box step to the assembled multitude, Mr. Jones. (COOPER *dances awkwardly by himself, as* VAN DAM *jerks him around or pokes him with his stick*)

COOPER (*to audience, in rhythm as he dances*): How could I
have done this? How could I have done this? Week by
week, year by year? Was this me, then? Was this really me,
then? (VAN DAM *pokes him*)

VAN DAM: And how do we hold our hands? (COOPER *holds his
hands out appropriately*)

COOPER: Is this what my roots are? This degrading ritual?
Week by week, year by year? (*Breaks out of the rhythm*)
Why didn't I protest against this drunken old fascist? My
own sons would have taken one look and headed for the
hills! Why didn't I rebel—like Stewart Granger in *SCARA-
MOUCHE*? (*Suddenly grabs* VAN DAM'*s stick, pretends to run
him through, stands over him triumphantly. The others clap.
But* VAN DAM *bounces to his feet*)

VAN DAM: One together, two together . . .

COOPER: Oh, but not me. Oh no! Me, I volunteered to be a
galley slave, like Ben Hur on a bad day. Why did I accept
it? Why did I keep going? (LUCY *enters on the side, carrying
a book, talking furtively on the telephone*)

LUCY: I can only talk a minute! They're watching me like
hawks. But I've managed to call all the old gang, and they
say they'll come out of the woodwork for the Snow Ball!

COOPER (*still in dancing school*): We'd look like fools without
Jack and Kitty.

LUCY: Slowly, Cooper! Gently! One step at a time, remember?
(*She goes off*)

VAN DAM (*simultaneously*): . . . One step at a time, remember? (KITTY PRICE *enters on the staircase, in a shining white dress. She is young and gorgeous—and is to be cast young, the only woman in the dancing class who is close to her stage age.* VAN DAM *sees her, raps his stick angrily on the ground. The music stops. Everyone looks at* KITTY)

KITTY: Ooops. Sorry I'm late.

VAN DAM: Indeed you are, Miss Price. It is becoming a habit with you.

KITTY: I guess I lost track of the time.

COOPER (*aside to* FRITZI): Watch this. He won't dare get mad at her.

FRITZI: Why not?

COOPER: She's the richest girl in town. If she quit, so would everybody else.

VAN DAM: We will overlook it this time, Miss Price. (COOPER *and* FRITZI *shake hands knowingly*) The young gentlemen may now ask the young ladies to dance. (*All the boys dash across the floor, and slide to a stop in front of* KITTY, *who beams proudly*) STOP! (*The boys do*) Go back! (*The boys return to their places*) The young gentlemen will ask the young ladies to dance. (*This time the boys move more slowly across the floor, elbowing each other out of the way.* COOPER *gets to* KITTY *first. In the process,* FRITZI *gets a nose bleed*)

BARBARA: Mr. Van Dam! Fritzi has a nose bleed!

VAN DAM: Oh please. (*He shoos them off*) Handkerchiefs out! A waltz please, Mr. Cromeier! (*The piano plays a slow waltz.* LUCY *and* LIZ *dance together*) Now the waltz is one two three, one two three . . .

LUCY (*to* LIZ): Don't you wish you were Kitty Price?

LIZ: Sometimes.

LUCY: I mean, she's both rich and beautiful.

LIZ: I know. But she's kind of lazy.

LUCY: What makes you say that?

LIZ: I sit next to her in arithmetic. She hardly knows how to divide.

LUCY: She doesn't need to divide. When you're that rich, all you have to do is multiply. (COOPER *dances with* KITTY)

COOPER: Will you come to Smithers drugstore afterwards? I'll buy you a soda.

KITTY: No thank you. I'm being driven straight home so no one will kidnap me.

COOPER: O.K. I'll meet you next Monday after school. I'll show you the zoo.

KITTY: No thanks. I find the monkey house generally embarrassing.

COOPER: Tell you what, then. You can watch me play hockey next Saturday afternoon.

KITTY: I can't. I'm going skiing with my father.

COOPER: Then when CAN I see you?

KITTY (*as he steps on her toe*): Ouch, Cooper! . . . Maybe when you become a better dancer.

VAN DAM: That is the waltz. . . . We will now take our seats for a slight collation. (JACK *enters, a young busboy in a white jacket, carrying glasses of pink punch on a silver tray. The boys and girls follow him off.* VAN DAM *exits as well, sneaking a furtive snort from his silver flask.* SAUL RADNER *enters as if into his office. He is a real estate developer, and wears a business suit. He calls* COOPER *off the dance floor*)

SAUL: Come on in, Coop. When do we start up our winter squash series?

COOPER: When you learn how to handle my serve.

SAUL: I've handled it for ten years, pal. I think you're scared of my corner shot.

COOPER: That does it! The clash of the Titans resumes next Tuesday! . . . Hey. Dig the new decor. Hard to believe this office once belonged to my old man. (*Picks up a fancy telephone*) Gimme Donald Trump! Gimme Barbra Streisand!

SAUL: Come work for us, and we'll put one of those in your car.

COOPER: No thanks, pal. No more downtown deals for me. I'll settle for selling houses to my people, as they retreat to the suburbs.

SAUL: That's a good one—your "people."

COOPER: Sure. We're kind of the lost tribe these days, Saul.

SAUL: Bullshit.

COOPER: I'm serious. I feel like an exile. This isn't my territory any more. All these new buildings. Even the old George Washington hotel is different.

SAUL: Except for one room.

COOPER: Except for one room.

SAUL: Your "people" on the Landmark Commission cost us a small fortune on that one.

COOPER: Actually that's why I'm here.

SAUL: I figured. (*Reads a letter on his desk*) Ms. Lucy Dunbar . . . wants to put on a . . . "Snow Ball."

COOPER: She said you turned her down.

SAUL: I didn't turn her DOWN, Coop. I asked her to broaden her base.

COOPER: Broaden her base?

SAUL: When you reopen a public facility, Coop, particularly when federal funds are involved, it's a good idea to kick things off a little more . . . well, democratically.

COOPER: Hey. The Snow Ball is open to anyone who wants to come.

SAUL (*referring to letter*): Anyone in "formal attire" holding a two-hundred buck ticket.

COOPER: That's for a New York orchestra and open bar and special decorations and . . .

SAUL: Forgive me, Coop, but some of our minority citizens might see it simply as the Old Guard doing their old number at taxpayers' expense.

COOPER: Oh come on . . .

SAUL: Open it up, Coop. Reflect the ethnic diversity in town. Less liquor, more food. Tacos, pizzas, egg rolls. Throw in a folk singer, maybe a rock group for the kids.

COOPER: That room was designed for ballroom dancing, Saul.

SAUL: I know that.

COOPER: My grandfather had that dance floor imported specially from Austria.

SAUL: I know, I know.

COOPER: Grover Cleveland danced in that room. Irene Castle danced there. Charles Van Dam taught dancing school there for almost fifty years.

SAUL: Coop, the Landmarks Committee gave us the whole history lesson . . .

COOPER: Well what's wrong with a little history now and then? Continuity? Tradition? You, of all people, should understand that. I'll bet if this were a fund-raiser for Israel, you'd be cheering us on.

SAUL: Now wait a minute.

COOPER: I want this, Saul. I want it. I put you up for the Tennis Club. I wrote that recommendation for your son to Williams. Now please. You do this for me. (*Pause*)

SAUL: Give your party, Coop.

COOPER: Thanks, Saul.

SAUL: Give your party.

COOPER: Now I assume you'll send us a good, healthy bill for the use of the room. We may be a lost tribe these days, but we still pay our own way.

SAUL: You sure? I hear your office lost out on that new mall.

COOPER: We're doing O.K.

SAUL: Seriously, Coop. Come work with me. Together we could get this burg back on its feet. And squeeze in some squash at lunch.

COOPER: Let's talk about it after the first of the year.

SAUL: You mean you're postponing a major career decision because of some *party?*

COOPER: Not a party, Saul. A dance. There's a big difference. This may even involve Jack and Kitty.

SAUL: Who and who?

COOPER: You and Rhoda come see. You're in for a big surprise.

SAUL: Sorry, Coop. We're booked that night. Flying over to Jerusalem for a major dinner party at the Wailing Wall. (SAUL *goes off, as the boys and girls reenter with* VAN DAM)

VAN DAM: Concentrate on your conversations, ladies and gentlemen. (JACK *comes down to* COOPER *with a tray of punch*)

JACK: Want some punch?

COOPER: Thanks.

JACK (*confidentially*): Say, could I speak to you privately a minute?

COOPER: Sure. (*They move away from the group*)

JACK: How do I get into this dancing school?

COOPER: Huh?

JACK: I've been watching from the kitchen. I already learned the steps. (*He gives a demonstration; he is good*)

COOPER: If you know already, why do you want to get in?

JACK: Personal reasons. (KITTY *comes down to* VAN DAM)

KITTY: Mr. Van Dam. I have to leave.

VAN DAM: The class is not over, Miss Price.

KITTY (*with a quick curtsy*): I know, but I think I've had enough for one evening. (*She bounces up the staircase*) Thanks! (*She goes out*)

JACK: That's the reason.

COOPER: Kitty?

JACK: I want to dance with *her*.

COOPER: You and the rest of the Free World.

JACK: So how do I get in?

COOPER: I don't know exactly. My mother has some list. You have to know people.

JACK: I know you.

COOPER: I don't know you.

JACK: I'm Jack Daley.

COOPER: Cooper Jones. . . . Hiya, Jack. (*They shake hands*) And I think you have to pay three hundred dollars.

JACK: I can come up with that.

COOPER: You can come up with three hundred *dollars?*

JACK: I saved it. Working here.

COOPER: Do you have a dark suit?

JACK: I'll get one.

COOPER: Then you definitely should get in. I mean, are we a democracy, or what? I'll ask my mother.

VAN DAM (*tapping his stick; with great distaste*): We will now undergo a lindy-hop. (*Everyone cheers;* VAN DAM *drinks*) Music, Mr. Cromeier, if you please. (*Music begins, a lively lindy*)

JACK (*dancing off with his tray*): Tell your mother I want to start next Saturday.

COOPER (*dancing with* LIZ): O.K., Jack Daley. (*To* LIZ) Stop leading. I'm the boy.

LIZ: Then lead, please.

COOPER: I'm trying to. But you keep going your own way.

LIZ: Why do you keep dancing with me, then?

COOPER: I'm practicing for the wrestling team.

VAN DAM: Change partners! (COOPER *switches to* LUCY)

LUCY: You dance beautifully, Cooper.

COOPER: Thanks.

LUCY: I'm serious. I can put myself completely into your hands.

COOPER: Thanks.

LUCY: And you'd be even better if you took that thing out of your pocket.

COOPER: What thing? Oh. Gosh. Sorry. (LUCY *dances off with the others as a waiter sets up a table with two coffee cups.* COOPER *calls off as he moves toward it*) Joe! If my secretary calls, tell her I'll be back in ten minutes. (LUCY *comes back on, in contemporary clothes. They settle at the table*)

LUCY: I've tracked them down.

COOPER: Jack and Kitty?

LUCY: Both. Since you seem to feel they're so essential.

COOPER: Yep. I do. They're the heart of the matter.

LUCY (*checking her notebook*): Jack is living in Indianapolis with wife and children.

COOPER: I knew that. He sends me a Christmas card every year.

LUCY: I'll bet you didn't know he's running for governor.

COOPER: Governor!

LUCY: According to my cousin, who lives there . . . (*Reads from her notes*) He's assistant district attorney now, and he's being seriously mentioned as the Republican candidate for Governor of Indiana!

COOPER: Good old Jack. Still moving on up . . .

LUCY (*consulting her notes*): And Kitty . . .

COOPER: Ah, Kitty . . .

LUCY: Kitty has married again.

COOPER: Again?

LUCY: Number three. A retired banker named Baldwin Hall. They live in this posh resort down in Florida.

COOPER: Oh boy. We've got our work cut out for us.

LUCY: Exactly. I think we should start by writing them both letters, just to break the ice.

COOPER: O.K. I'll write Jack. You write Kitty.

LUCY: Fine.

COOPER: And tell Kitty I have the music.

LUCY: The music?

COOPER: The musical arrangements. From the Snow Ball. Jack gave them to me when they split up. (*Calls as if for bill*) Joe!

LUCY: And you kept them? All these years? I *knew* you were a closet romantic, Cooper Jones. (*She pokes him with her pencil*)

COOPER: Tell Kitty I'll Xerox them, and send them on. (*They get up from the table;* COOPER *leaves money*)

LUCY: We should work out a budget.

COOPER: Yes.

LUCY: I'm hopeless at budgets. Gordon did all that.

COOPER: Oh budgets aren't so difficult.

LUCY: Then stop by tonight and show me, step by step.

COOPER: Can't. It's Liz's birthday.

LUCY: Oh. Well. Far be it from me to intrude on THAT. . . .

(*The music and lights come up as the class reenters. Again the dancing has improved.* JACK *dances with* BARBARA FISKE)

BARBARA: Don't you love dancing cheek to cheek, Jack?

JACK: I don't know. It gets a little sweaty, maybe.

BARBARA: I like that. I think it's sexy.

JACK: I dunno. I think I'm getting a rash. (COOPER *and* LUCY *are back in by now.* KITTY *enters down the stairs.* VAN DAM *sees her and once again raps for order. The music stops*)

KITTY: I know, I know. I'm late again. (*She looks around*) Gulp.

VAN DAM: I believe everyone has found a partner, Miss Price.

KITTY: Then I'll just sit this one out. (*She sits*)

VAN DAM: Miss Price! (*He approaches her*) Perhaps you would like to dance with *me*.

KITTY: You?

VAN DAM (*he bows to her*): May I have this dance? (KITTY *does not rise and curtsy*)

LIZ (*aside to* HEATHER): The old letch.

HEATHER: What will she DO?

VAN DAM (*he holds out his arms to* KITTY): Music, Mr. Cromeier, if you pl—

JACK (*suddenly*): I'll dance with her.

VAN DAM: I believe you already have a partner, Mr. . . . ah . . . Mr. . . .

JACK: Daley.

VAN DAM: I believe you are already dancing with Miss Fiske.

JACK: No offense, but she doesn't get the beat. She can't follow me at all. (BARBARA *bursts into tears, and runs to the other girls, who comfort her*) Tell you what: *you* dance with Miss Fiske. *I'll* dance with Miss Price. (*General uproar.* VAN DAM *gets order by pounding on the floor with his stick*)

VAN DAM: No. I'll tell *you* what, Mr. . . . ah . . . Daley. You will dance with Miss Price. And the rest of us will take our seats and watch.

JACK: O.K.

VAN DAM: And let me add, Mr. Daley, that you had better be very, very good!

KITTY (*to the other girls*): Eeeek.

VAN DAM: Mr. Cromeier, if you please . . . a rumba.

KITTY: A RUMBA? Hey, no fair! We haven't even learned that one!

VAN DAM: Ah, but Mr. Daley will teach you.

KITTY: Yipes.

VAN DAM: Be seated, everyone. . . . Music, Mr. Cromeier, if
you please. (*Music: a rumba.* JACK *gives* KITTY *a beautiful,
deep bow.* KITTY *responds with a dramatic, ironic parody of
a curtsy. The handkerchief comes out, and then they dance.
They dance tentatively at first, finding the beat,* JACK *taking
the lead,* KITTY *following, always with a wry little shrug, and
always a little bit late. They learn as they go along, and as
they learn they get trickier, trying this and that, and the
music seems to respond and take fire from what they do. The
boys and girls cheer them on, so that* VAN DAM *has to tap his
stick and yell, "Settle down! Settle down!" Soon* JACK *and
*KITTY *are looking pretty good, building finally to an elaborate
coda, where he spins her off in a lovely flourish, and ends
the dance with a deep theatrical bow. Everyone applauds.
The boys all gather enthusiastically around* JACK, *and bring
him downstage, as the girls gather around* KITTY *and propel
her off.* MR. SMITHERS, *a druggist in a white jacket, sets up a
counter as* VAN DAM *exits, taking a nip from his flask. The
boys do a lot of whooping and cheering and backslapping as
they settle in around the table*)

COOPER: I'm paying for Jack. I got a dollar for shovelling snow.

BILLY: That's not all you shovel, Cooper. (*Roars of laughter*)

SMITHERS: What'll it be, boys?

COOPER: You got that new chocolate chip ice cream?

CALVIN: You got cherry phosphates?

FRITZI: You got Prince Albert in the can? If so, let him out!
(*More roars of laughter*)

BILLY: When we heard the sirens and saw the patrols We
knew it was Smithers for whom the bell tolls. (*Laughter*)

CALVIN: Hey, Mr. Smithers! Have you got that new paper-
back, *The Tiger's Revenge*, by Claude Balls? (*Laughter*)

SMITHERS: All right, boys. Settle down, settle down. (*He goes
off*)

COOPER: Say, you're a terrific dancer, Jack! (*Other boys echo
approval: Fred Astaire! Gene Kelly!*)

JACK: Thanks for getting me into dancing school.

BILLY: *Thanks?* You said *thanks?* You mean you *wanted* to go?

COOPER: He wanted to dance with Kitty.

CALVIN: I dunno. I don't think even Kitty is worth going to
dancing school for.

JACK: I had another reason, too. I figure dancing school will
be good for my future.

FRITZI: Your *future?*

JACK: Sure. You learn things in dancing school. You learn man-
ners. You learn clothes. You learn how to talk to people
when you don't give a shit.

Jack Daley and Kitty Price

All photos of the 1991 Old Globe Theatre (San Diego, California) production by Ken Howard.

Jack and Kitty perform for Mr. Van Dam and the dancing class.

Cooper, Liz and Lucy

Jack and Kitty as they are before Jack and Kitty as they were.

FRITZI: That's true . . .

JACK: Sure. And you meet people. Getting to know you people will help me succeed in life. I figure it's worth three hundred dollars.

BILLY: You mean you're PAYING for it? With your OWN money?

JACK: Sure. I saved it for my college education, but I decided this was an equally important investment. (SMITHERS *returns*)

SMITHERS: Who here is Jack Daley? (*Everyone: Ta-da, pointing out* JACK)

JACK: Me. Why?

SMITHERS: There's a fellow in a uniform asking to see you.

FRITZI: Jiggers. The cops.

CALVIN: You rob a bank for that three hundred, Jack?

COOPER (*looking out*): That's no cop! That's a chauffeur. . . . And Kitty's father's sitting in the back of the car.

ALL: Uh oh.

SMITHERS: He wants to meet you, son.

JACK: O.K.! (*Runs off jauntily*) So long, suckers!

CALVIN (*looking out*): This I gotta see!

BILLY: It's one of those new Lincoln Continentals!

COOPER: They're shaking hands!

BILLY: He's getting in!

COOPER: They're driving off!

FRITZI (*producing a schoolbook, with a brown paper cover*): Hey! Jack forgot his book.

COOPER: What book?

FRITZI: This book he studies on the bus.

COOPER (*taking it, reading the cover*): Tenth Grade Civics. Holy Angels Collegiate Institute. (*Reads inside*) *How Democracy Works.*

BILLY (*looking after* JACK): It sure is working for *him*. (*The boys go off, leaving* COOPER. *Restaurant music comes up. The lights become more romantic. A* WAITER *brings on a table with a cloth and a candlestick.* LIZ *comes in, breathlessly late, wearing an overcoat. She kisses him*)

LIZ: Sorry, sweetheart. . . . What with a late meeting, and the snow, and . . .

COOPER (*helping with her coat, which the* WAITER *takes*): Happy Birthday . . . (*He gives her a warm kiss*)

LIZ: Thanks. (*She settles in*) Susie called as I was going out the door. She wants to stay at college over Thanksgiving, and put her travel money toward a used car.

COOPER: No.

LIZ: That's exactly what I said. No.

COOPER: The children come home, Thanksgiving and Christmas. That's absolutely non-negotiable.

LIZ: I couldn't agree more.

COOPER: Can you imagine you and me, all by ourselves, eyeing each other over a Thanksgiving turkey?

LIZ: I suppose we'll have to face that some day.

COOPER: Not if I can help it. (WAITER *reappears*)

WAITER: A cocktail, madam?

LIZ: Just club soda, please.

COOPER (*indicating his own drink*): You won't join me?

LIZ: No thanks.

COOPER: How about champagne? On your birthday?

LIZ: Champagne gives me a headache. (*To* WAITER) Just club soda, please. (WAITER *goes off*)

COOPER: I've decided on your present.

LIZ: Oh yes?

COOPER: You've got to pick it out.

LIZ: I hope it's not jewelry, Cooper. I can't wander around town, dripping with jewels, while people are sleeping in the streets.

COOPER: It's not jewelry. . . . It's a new dress.

LIZ: Cooper, I'm not sure I need a . . .

COOPER: A long dress. For the Snow Ball.

LIZ: Oh.

COOPER: I checked out Berger's. I saw a great dress there. The salesgirl held it up. You'd look sensational in it.

LIZ: Describe it.

COOPER: Well, it has a . . . and a little . . . oh hell, it's dark green. You'll have to go see.

LIZ: How much?

COOPER: Never mind.

LIZ: How MUCH, Cooper?

COOPER: Four hundred smackeroos.

LIZ: Four *hundred* dollars?

COOPER: Including tax.

LIZ: That is outrageous! To pay four hundred dollars for some dumb dress, when the library closes three days a week! (*The* WAITER *shows up with the seltzer*) Nope. Sorry. I'll wear some old rag, thanks . . . I suppose we should order. (*She looks at the menu*)

COOPER: I've already ordered. Something special.

LIZ: What?

COOPER: Rack of lamb.

LIZ: Lamb?

COOPER: And fresh asparagus.

LIZ: Sweetheart, lamb is saturated with fat.

COOPER: It is not.

LIZ: Darling, it's oozing with it. And do you know what they do to these baby lambs in order to—

COOPER: Oh Liz . . .

LIZ (*to* WAITER): Could I just have the . . . I don't know . . . scrod, broiled, no butter, and a small green salad with dressing on the side.

WAITER: Certainly, madam.

COOPER: I'll have the goddam lamb.

WAITER (to COOPER): What about the soufflé, sir?

COOPER (to LIZ): I ordered the grand marnier soufflé for dessert.

LIZ: Oh that sounds wonderful! (To WAITER) I'll have a taste of his.

WAITER: A single soufflé then?

COOPER: A single soufflé.

LIZ: And herb tea, for me.

COOPER: Not even decaf?

LIZ: Do you know what those coffee companies pay their peasants in Peru?

COOPER: Help. (The WAITER goes off)

LIZ: The reason I was late was we had this knock-down, drag-out meeting at the office. They want to give the holiday party down at the Community Center the Saturday after Christmas.

COOPER: But that's the night of the Snow Ball!

LIZ: I KNOW, darling. I fought it tooth and nail. But it's the best date for everyone else.

COOPER: So what gives? You're not coming to the Snow Ball?

LIZ: I'll just have to make a showing at both.

COOPER: Say you've got a previous engagement. You've done it before.

LIZ: I can't this time, sweetheart . . . I've been promoted.

COOPER: No kidding! When?

LIZ: Last week.

COOPER: Why didn't you tell me?

LIZ: Because I was nervous about what you'd say.

COOPER: What I'd say?

LIZ: It'll take much more time.

COOPER: Will you come home Thanksgiving and Christmas?

LIZ: See? That's what I was nervous about.

COOPER: No, seriously. Congratulations! (*Kisses her*) What's your title?

LIZ: I am now known as a Family Interventionist. I intervene, when necessary.

COOPER: You'll be great at that.

LIZ: Well, we could use the dough, sweetie. With the kids in college and all.

COOPER: Right. So. For your birthday, what would you like? Is there an Interventionist's Handbook? Or how about a four-volume history of the Marshall Plan? Name it. It's yours.

LIZ: No, listen, here's what I'd really like. Computer lessons. To learn how to work one of those things. I could use it in the office, and maybe get one for home, and I could get twice as much done in half the time . . . (*The lights fade on* LIZ, *as she talks, and come up on* LUCY, *across the stage, sitting at a bar, with two glasses of white wine in front of her. She hails* COOPER)

LUCY: Hey! Yoo-hoo! Over here! (COOPER *crosses to her*)

COOPER (*glancing around*): Hey, how'd you find this joint? The Half Moon Bar and Grille?

LUCY: Where else should we meet? Your precious Club? With everyone breathing down our necks? No thanks. It's time you branched out a little, Cooper Jones. (*Indicating the wine*) And I've already ordered you a drink.

COOPER: In the middle of the day?

LUCY: Absolutely. I think you and I should spend this entire snowy afternoon stuffing our faces with greasy chicken wings and getting pleasantly polluted.

COOPER (*sitting beside her*): What's the trouble?

LUCY: My job, for one thing. They just chewed me out for talking to the customers. They say I flirt with the men.

COOPER (*mock horror*): What? You? I don't believe it.

LUCY: I like men. I like talking about books. I don't know why I can't combine the two.

COOPER: Why don't you quit?

LUCY: Money, Cooper. Believe it or not, there are some people in the world who need it. Besides, it's a place to go. Anyway, look what finally arrived from Kitty.

COOPER: Better late than never.

LUCY: Not when you read what she says.

COOPER (*reading*): "I couldn't possibly drag Baldwin north in the dead of winter . . ."

LUCY: Baldwin's her husband.

COOPER: "And we're expecting a houseful of children and step-children and grandchildren over Christmas vacation . . ."

LUCY: See?

COOPER: Shit.

LUCY: And, to make things worse, Jane Babcock tells me she just ran into her at the Mayo Clinic. She was having tests. Jane didn't dare bring up the Snow Ball.

COOPER: Hell.

LUCY: So that's that. . . . Anything new from Jack?

COOPER: Just what I told you. I wrote two letters, and got two polite put-downs from some assistant in his office.

LUCY: So where are we?

COOPER: Nowhere. (*He stares at* KITTY's *note*)

LUCY: So. Let's talk about books. What have you read lately? *The Decline of the Wasp?*

COOPER (*rereading* KITTY's *note*): Hey!

LUCY: What?

COOPER: Did you read this last sentence?

LUCY: What?

COOPER (*reading*): ". . . Just think. Another Snow Ball. Jeez Louise. My heart automatically goes thumpety-thump . . ."

LUCY: Typical Kitty.

COOPER: She's giving us an opening, Lucy.

LUCY: The size of a pin-hole.

COOPER: She is beckoning to us. She is calling. She's saying tell me more.

LUCY: Oh Cooper . . .

COOPER: I sense it. I feel it in my bones.

LUCY: So what do we do?

COOPER: We telephone them both. Immediately.

LUCY: You mean just . . .

COOPER: Call them up. Person to person. Tell each one that the other is on the fence.

LUCY: But that wouldn't be . . .

COOPER: All's fair in love and dancing! I'll call Jack, you call Kitty.

LUCY: Heavens, Cooper. You certainly are taking the bit in your teeth.

COOPER: Faint heart ne'er won fair lady.

LUCY: But if she's sick?

COOPER: If she says so, we'll back right off. (*Gets up*) Come on. We'll go over to my office and telephone.

LUCY: Could we make it my place?

COOPER: Why?

LUCY: I'm expecting a call. From Minneapolis. From this man. Well I mean, he's a welcome change from that prick who held me hostage for twenty years. (*Pause*) He keeps wanting to marry me.

COOPER: And why don't you?

LUCY: Because he's not . . . I mean, he wouldn't . . . I mean, something like the Snow Ball is totally out of his league.

COOPER: Ah hah.

LUCY: So. Let's go to my place. If Minneapolis calls, I'll say I'm otherwise engaged. (*Pause*)

COOPER: I have to show a house this afternoon.

LUCY: Oh well. A house . . .

COOPER: Money, Lucy. Remember? I haven't been holding my end up at the office lately.

LUCY: Oh well. I wouldn't want to take bread from the mouths of your children. We'll call separately. (COOPER *puts down money*) No, no. My turn. (LUCY *puts her money on top of his; their hands touch and stay touching*) After all, we're both in this thing together.

COOPER (*bowing and offering his arm*): Shall we dance?

LUCY (*curtsying*): You must have gone to dancing school, sir. Which is more than I can say for my man from Minneapolis. (*She goes off.* COOPER *turns to the audience*)

COOPER (*to audience*): It wasn't that great, actually. Not at the start. Maybe because it really wasn't about us. It was all about Jack and Kitty. They were on our minds that afternoon, and those other afternoons when we met again. It was as if we were just the subplot, two minor characters marking time, until the stars were ready to come on and play their big scene. (LUCY *comes on dressed informally*)

LUCY: I just thought you should know: Ruthie Curtis saw Kitty at Bergdorf's in New York. Buying an evening dress!

COOPER: For the Snow Ball?

LUCY: She wouldn't say. But it was not the sort of thing you'd wear to some golf club in Florida! (*They kiss*)

COOPER: I finally got through to Jack. He said he hasn't danced in thirty years.

LUCY: Did you tell him it will come back?

COOPER: I said it was like riding a bicycle.

LUCY: Exactly. Like that, or other things. (*They kiss more passionately; then* LUCY *breaks away*) Hey! Slow down. I'm right in the middle of a good book.

COOPER: What book?

LUCY: *Lady Chatterley's Lover.* (*She goes off invitingly.* COOPER *turns to the audience again*)

COOPER: So things got better, as we got closer to the Snow Ball. Jack and Kitty were still on the fence, but we began to feel that by making love, we could copulate them into commitment. In our more lurid moments, we even joked about it. We called it "Snowballing" . . . (SAUL RADNER *crosses the stage, in shirtsleeves, carrying a squash racquet, drying his hair with a towel*)

SAUL: Good game, Coop. You're hotter than a pistol these days.

COOPER: Thanks, Saul.

SAUL: You been exercising on the sly?

COOPER: No, no. Just generally keeping fit.

SAUL: No, it's more than that. You seem like a guy who's got a girl somewhere. (COOPER *laughs nervously as* SAUL *goes off, passing* LIZ *on the way in*)

LIZ (*holding a little pink note*): Look what I got in the mail!

COOPER: What?

LIZ: An anonymous note. "Interventionist: intervene thyself."

COOPER: Some crank. Some weirdo from your work.

LIZ: On pink writing paper? With that little face at the end? It's someone we know.

COOPER: But the grammar's wrong. Intervene is an intransitive verb. It should be "intervene *on* thyself." Or "*with* thyself." It's some uneducated kook.

LIZ: At least it has a Biblical ring . . . I'll look it up in Bartlett's . . . (*She goes off*)

COOPER (*looking after her; then to audience*): Oh God, what a shit I am! What a shit! Because I love her! I love her even when I argue with her. I love her even *because* I argue with her. She keeps life interesting every minute of the day. As for Lucy, do I love her, too? Or are we just hung up on the Snow Ball? Am I another one of those menopausal men, desperately trying to turn back the clock before the last alarm goes off? (LUCY *comes out, in a negligee*)

LUCY: Where've you been?

COOPER: Kitty's husband called me at the office.

LUCY: And?

JACK: She's in the hospital. For an operation.

LUCY: Oh no.

COOPER: I telephoned Jack, and he immediately backed off.

LUCY: Oh no!

COOPER: I wonder if we should back off, too.

LUCY: I know what you mean.

COOPER: I keep thinking of Liz.

LUCY: And the man from Minneapolis.

COOPER: The Snow Ball should keep rolling, of course.

LUCY: Of course. We'll just have to go through the motions.

COOPER: Well. I ought to get back. One of our kids is home for
the weekend.

LUCY: Oh then definitely you should go.

COOPER: So long, then, Lucy. (*Kisses her on the cheek*)

LUCY: Goodbye, Cooper. (*He starts out*) Cooper . . . will you
still dance with me at the Snow Ball?

COOPER: Of course I will, Lucy.

LUCY: I mean, we may not be Jack and Kitty, but I'd hate to
think we spent all those years dancing for nothing.

COOPER: Oh something will come of this. I'm sure of that.

(*They go off either way, as: the music comes up, bouncily, and
plays continuously. Decorations swing into place. We are now
at a series of parties, spanning several years. The boys are now*

in tuxedos, the girls in long dresses. A couple dances by; the girl is in a strapless dress)

BREWSTER: How come they call this a coming-out party?

HEATHER *(hoisting up her front)*: Wait till the conga, and you'll see. *(*JACK *and* KITTY *dance by, beautifully. Another couple watches)*

GINNY: I hear Jack Daley quit that Holy Angels parochial school, and is now going to Country Day.

BILLY: That's right. Kitty's father got him a full scholarship.

GINNY: My Lord! Is he doing well?

BILLY: Straight A's! And Co-captain on the football team!

GINNY *(suddenly kissing him)*: Oh, that Jack! He makes me proud to be an American. *(*JACK *and* KITTY *dance by again; people applaud as they dance off. Two boys, with drinks, cross)*

CALVIN *(confidentially)*: I saw Jack last Friday night, out with another girl.

FRITZI: Probably Terri Tolentino, his old girl from Holy Angels.

CALVIN: I thought Jack stayed in, Fridays, to do his homework.

FRITZI *(lewdly)*: He stays in Fridays, all right. He stays in all night long. *(Quickly; as* JACK *dances on with* LUCY*)* Hi, Jack.

JACK: Guys. (JACK *and* LUCY *dance*)

LUCY: You're a beautiful dancer, Jack.

JACK: Thanks, Lucy.

LUCY: No, you are. You're fabulous.

JACK: Thanks a lot. (COOPER *cuts in on* JACK *and* LUCY. JACK *goes off. Music continues.* COOPER *dances with* LUCY)

LUCY: You're a beautiful dancer, Cooper.

COOPER: Thank you, Lucy.

LUCY: I hear Liz doesn't like you to dance with me.

COOPER: She thinks I'm a pushover for your line.

LUCY: Line? What line? I don't have a line. (CALVIN *cuts in*)

COOPER: That's what I told her. (*He goes off*)

LUCY (*to* CALVIN, *who dances terribly*): You're a beautiful dancer, by the way.

CALVIN: Hey, thanks. (*They dance off.* JACK *joins* COOPER *in the men's room.* COOPER *stands at the "urinal."* JACK *combs his hair in a "mirror."*)

JACK: Look at you, Cooper. You're a slob. Your pants don't even fit.

COOPER: That's because this tux belonged to my grandfather.

JACK: I got mine tailor-made. It cost a mint, but I'm buying it on time.

COOPER: Hey, I could have lent you my older brother's.

JACK: No thanks. A man's clothes should fit. If your clothes fit, you feel fit. And if you feel fit, you dance well.

COOPER: And if you dance well? What then?

JACK: Oh well, my God, then the sky's the limit! (*They go off either way.* KITTY, HEATHER *and* GINNY *come into the ladies room.* KITTY *adjusts her dress*)

HEATHER (*from "stall"*): There's a boy here from Princeton who says he loves me.

KITTY: Don't believe him.

GINNY (*from next "stall"*): And this guy from Amherst wants to pin me.

KITTY: Watch it. He'll pin you to the ground.

HEATHER (*as they wash their hands*): Oh God! How do you tell if a man's sincere?

KITTY: Dance with him. Let him lead. You can tell immediately. (*She goes off; the girls look at each other and go off the opposite way.* JACK *dances with* LIZ)

LIZ: Congratulations, Jack. I hear you got into Harvard.

JACK: Right. And they gave me this great scholarship. Instead of waiting on tables, they want me to dance with Kitty at Alumni functions.

LIZ: That's terrific!

JACK: We'll be what the Whiffenpoofs are for Yale!

LIZ: What about Kitty? Where does she stand in all this?

JACK: Oh she's with me all the way. She's found a college near Harvard which gives lab credit for dancing. (*They dance off.* BREWSTER *and* HEATHER *dance by*)

BOY: Do you think Jack and Kitty are sleeping with each other?

GIRL: I don't think it's any of our business.

BOY: I hear they spent all last weekend down at Niagara Falls in the Maid of the Mist Motel.

GIRL: Honestly, Charlie! May we change the subject, please?

BOY: Sure. Go ahead.

GIRL: All right. Now. Here's the thing. I think I'm pregnant. (*They dance.* COOPER *and* KITTY *dance by*)

COOPER: When we were little kids, I was in love with you.

KITTY: You were not.

COOPER: I was! I thought you were the cat's ass.

KITTY: I love that expression!

COOPER: I still dream about you sometimes.

KITTY: That's because we're such good old friends.

COOPER: Say, how about coming skiing with me over New Year's?

KITTY: Can't, sweetie. I'll be with Jack.

COOPER: Thank God. I've already invited Liz.

KITTY: What would you have done if I'd said yes?

COOPER: Asked Lucy Dunbar to join us. (*Both laugh*) Do you love Jack, Kitty?

KITTY: Oh Cooper, I don't know.

COOPER: He's good for you, Kitty. He's given you something to go for.

KITTY: I know. (*She does a little spin*) But it's hard WORK being Ginger Rogers.

COOPER (*imitating*): It's no cinch being Jimmy Stewart, either. (GINNY *and* MARY *settle at a table. They have white ballots, white envelopes and white pencils*)

GINNY: This is agony . . . who are you going to vote for, for Snow Queen?

MARY: I think I'll vote for Kitty.

GINNY: But she's so anti-social. She's spent almost the entire vacation down in her rumpus room, alone with Jack.

MARY: Maybe she should just be Maid of Honor. (BARBARA *joins them*)

BARBARA: I'm voting for Agnes Underhill.

GINNY: But Agnes has that gimpy leg. And that horrible skin problem.

BARBARA: I know, but she deserves a sympathy vote. Besides, her cat just died. (*They vote carefully, hiding their ballots from each other*)

GINNY: Oh God. These decisions. I'm just not sure democracy's worth it. (*They go out.* COOPER *crosses with* LIZ)

COOPER: I voted for you for Snow Queen.

LIZ: You sure you didn't sneak one in for Lucy Dunbar?

COOPER: No, I swear. You're Queen to me, all the way.

LIZ: Whatever that means.

COOPER: I guess it means I'm asking you to go steady.

LIZ: Cooper—Gosh. Let me think about that.

COOPER: Let me know at the Snow Ball. (*She goes off as he turns to the audience*) Because it all came down to the Snow Ball. This was the only party you had to pay for, but the profits went to some good cause, and besides, you could always stick your grandmother for the bill. Balls are balls, as my father says, but the climax of this one, like the parading of the Virgin in an Italian street festival, was the presentation of the Snow Queen to the assembled multitude. (*A fanfare.* VAN DAM *comes down the staircase with a mike on a cord*)

VAN DAM: Ladies and gentlemen: it is my great pleasure to present to you . . . this year's Queen and her court. The beautiful Miss Kitty Price and her two lovely Maids of Honor. (*A drum roll. A spotlight on an entrance as* KITTY *is wheeled on in an elaborate sleigh. She wears a crown, and holds flowers.* LIZ *and* LUCY *sit below her, as Maids of Honor.* COOPER *and three other boys pull the sleigh around, as the band plays a swing version of a Christmas song, and everyone applauds. Over the mike*) Prance, gentlemen! Prance! You're supposed to be reindeer! (*The sleigh finally lurches to a stop in the center of the floor. More applause*)

KITTY (*holds up her hand to speak*): I just want everyone to know this thing is held up primarily by faith in God and Bergdorf Goodman. (*Laughter*)

VAN DAM (*holding up his hand*): Ladies and gentlemen: I'd also like a word, please. It has long been observed, by people wiser than myself, that every American city requires two things to keep it civilized: it must have a park, and it must have a dancing school. For forty-six years, I have been somewhat involved in the latter. (*Laughter and applause*) This year, however, will be my last. (*Genial protests*) No, no. My last. Because during the course of this year, I have enjoyed the rare pleasure of seeing my labors bear fruit. I have seen the dancing of Mr. Jack Daley and Miss Kitty Price. (*Cheers and applause*) The escorts will now ask the Queen and her court to dance. (COOPER *goes up, bows to* LIZ, *helps her out of the sleigh*)

COOPER: So? Are we going steady?

LIZ: Yes, Cooper. If you mean it seriously.

COOPER: Of course I do.

LIZ: Well let's hope. (*Another boy escorts* LUCY. KITTY *remains seated in the sleigh*)

GINNY: Kitty doesn't have a partner!

BILLY: Where's Jack?

BARBARA: Who knows?

FRITZI: Maybe he's over at Terry Tolentino's.

HEATHER: This is embarrassing. Kitty'll have to dance with her father.

VAN DAM (*on mike*): I notice our lovely Queen remains unattended. Perhaps, for my last Snow Ball, I might finally have the pleasure of dancing with her myself.

LIZ (*to someone*): He's still an old letch. (*General confusion.*
VAN DAM *goes to bow to* KITTY *in the sled*) May I have this
dance, Miss Price?

KITTY: Um . . . (*And everyone freezes*)

COOPER (*to audience*): Jack, of course, had arranged this whole
moment. He wanted the suspense. He had ordered music
specially arranged in New York, and dug up some guy who
did the lighting for Ringling Brothers, and now he was
waiting offstage, ready to make his move.

BILLY: There's Jack. In the orchestra.

MARY: Thank God!

GINNY: He's handing out sheet music. (JACK *comes on. He nods
as if to the orchestra. A long drum roll. He signals to the
flies. The lights dim, except for two gorgeous pink spotlights,
which hit him and* KITTY. *The drum roll continues. The other
dancers back off.* JACK *goes to the sleigh, bows to* KITTY, *holds
out his hand, helping her out. She steps down and gives her
bemused curtsy.* JACK *signals to two boys who ease the sleigh
out of the way. Then* JACK *gestures again toward the orchestra*) Hit it, Eddie! (*The band strikes up a snappy arrange-
ment of dance tunes, and* JACK *and* KITTY *launch into a terrific
number. They have obviously worked on it carefully, and
both the lights and the musical arrangements support what
they do*)

BILLY (*on the sidelines*): No fair. That's cheating. They've been
practicing to their own music.

GINNY: So *that's* what they were doing down in Kitty's rumpus
room.

LIZ (*to* COOPER): I still think she's lazy. Notice how she's always
a little late.

COOPER: At least she *follows* him.

LIZ: That's because he knows where he wants to go. (*The
dance modulates into a slower tempo.* COOPER *and* LUCY *exit
unobtrusively*)

FRITZI (*watching the dancers*): Poetry in motion, that's what it
is. Poetry in motion.

GINNY: If they wore skates, they could be in the Olympics.

FRITZI: They make the hair stand up on the back of my neck.

CALVIN: You said that yesterday about the new Thunderbird.

(JACK *and* KITTY's *dance builds. They might dance up the staircase, and freeze on the balustrade.* COOPER *and* LUCY, *both now
in contemporary overcoats, enter from either side. They meet
somewhere in the center, isolated in light*)

COOPER: I got your message.

LUCY: Kitty telephoned. She's out of the hospital, and now
wants to come more than ever!

COOPER: I'll call Jack immediately! . . . We've done it,
haven't we?

LUCY: We're bringing it all back home.

COOPER: Lucy, I want to sleep with you all night long!

LUCY: What about Liz?

COOPER: I'll tell her I got stuck in the snow. (*They kiss passionately, and go up the stairs, as* JACK *and* KITTY *dance down, building their dance to a rousing climax. At the end, everyone gathers in on them, applauding, including* COOPER *and* LUCY, *who have had time to reenter as their young selves*)

END OF ACT ONE

ACT TWO ***

✽✽✽ ACT TWO ✽✽✽

The Cotillion Room is bustling with preparations for the revival of the Snow Ball. Someone is setting up tables, LUCY *and others are on stepladders in work clothes, stringing up a large sign: "WELCOME BACK, KITTY AND JACK!"* COOPER *addresses the audience.*

COOPER (*to audience*): . . . And so the day arrived. There were articles in the paper, interviews on TV, and a special exhibit at the historical society with pictures of Jack and Kitty, and taped interviews of people who had seen them dance . . .

(BREWSTER, *who has been working on the decorations, calls to another*)

BREWSTER: Question for a fellow sports fan.

BILLY: Yo.

BREWSTER: How many times did Jack and Kitty dance, during their final season together?

BILLY: Are we talking home, or away?

BREWSTER: Both, naturally.

BILLY: Twenty-seven times, according to the latest statistics.

BREWSTER: Wrong. Twenty-nine. They danced twice in Toronto.

BILLY: Canada? We're counting Canada now? Since when do we count Canada?

COOPER (to audience): We became the hottest ticket in town
. . . (SAUL comes up to him)

SAUL: Hey, Coop, can you do me a favor? I need two tickets
tonight for me and Rhoda.

COOPER: We're sold out, pal. Sorry.

SAUL: Couldn't you squeeze us in? I'll pay for it. Extra.

COOPER: Tell you what, Saul. We're setting up bleachers in
back. Give your name to Mrs. Klinger.

SAUL: Bleachers? For Rhoda? You must be mad.

COOPER: Or . . .

SAUL: Or what?

COOPER: You could help underwrite a Sponsor's Table.

SAUL: That's blackmail, Coop. But I'll call you. (He goes out)

COOPER (to audience): I wish I could say the day dawned
bright and clear. But it didn't. It dawned damp and gray.
And we all knew, without knowing we knew, that we were
in for a major snow storm . . . (LIZ comes on, in parka and
boots, carrying COOPER's tuxedo in a plastic bag)

LIZ: Here's your stuff, Cooper. Tux, shirt, studs, everything.

COOPER: Thanks. I'll change in the men's room.

LIZ: That tuxedo cost a small fortune to repair, by the way. It was riddled with moth holes.

COOPER: Just as long as it fits.

LIZ: It never did, remember?

COOPER: What's it like outside?

LIZ: Beginning to snow. I wonder if they'll make it.

COOPER: They'll make it. What's a little snow between friends?

LIZ: See you later, then. (*She starts off, then stops, calls up to* LUCY, *who's still on ladder*) Hey, is that sign fireproof?

LUCY: Of course, Liz.

LIZ: Are you sure? These manufacturers get away with murder these days.

COOPER: It's O.K., Liz.

LIZ: Well I'm worried about people who smoke. I think you should rope them off, at the far end of the room.

LUCY: We're not going to do that, Liz.

COOPER: It's O.K., Lucy.

LUCY: Anyway, why do you care, Liz? I hear you have another party on your agenda tonight.

LIZ: Right. Over at the Community Center. (*Rhythmically*)
  Tell Jack and Kitty to forget this fuss,
  For some free-style rap dancing over with us.

(*She executes a step, and goes out*)

LUCY (*coming down off the ladder*): She hates me, doesn't she?

COOPER: Naw.

LUCY: She wouldn't look at me.

COOPER: She's got a lot on her mind.

LUCY: She's got *us* on her mind.

COOPER: I wish she did.

LUCY: What does that mean?

COOPER: Skip it.

LUCY: Tell her, Cooper.

COOPER: Tell her what?

LUCY: Everything. That we love each other, and want to get
  married.

COOPER: I will.

LUCY: You keep saying that, but you don't.

COOPER: I'm waiting for the right time.

LUCY: Tell her tonight.

COOPER: Tonight?

LUCY: After the Snow Ball. To clear the air.

COOPER: I can't just take my wife home after a festive occasion, and tell her I'm leaving.

LUCY: Cooper, I am out on a limb here! I just got fired because of this goddam "festive occasion!"

COOPER: What?

LUCY: They noticed the telephone bill . . . all those long distance calls to Kitty.

COOPER: Oh boy.

LUCY: Oh well. I can still call Minneapolis.

COOPER: Hey look . . .

LUCY: I'm serious, Cooper. Tonight's the night. Now bite the bullet. Or get off the pot. (*She goes out*)

COOPER (*to audience*): Oh God! Can a man be in love with two women at the same time? Which way do I turn? Lucy, with her satin nightgowns, and agreeable ways, and spectacular behavior in bed—Oh Lucy, I'm young again when I'm with you! She's found this cozy little carriage house off in the woods, and is already thumbing through the Laura Ashley catalogue. Why shouldn't I settle there, and listen to good old songs, and read good old books and watch *Masterpiece Theatre* on Sunday nights? What's wrong with that? . . . Of course, there's Liz. Impossible Liz. Fighting her past, fighting the world, fighting ME, all the way to the finish. Only after we're dead will I get off the hook. Then I can relax. In hell, with all the other adulterers. While Liz goes straight to heaven. Of course once she's there, I'm sure she'll spend most of her time getting God to register as a Democrat. (A MUSICIAN *comes up to* COOPER; *he carries a clarinet*)

MUSICIAN: Mr. Jones, we're ready to rehearse in the back room.

COOPER (*getting a stack of music; to* MUSICIAN): Could you start by running through these arrangements? Because of the snow, the dancers might be a little late.

MUSICIAN (*looking them over*): Hey, this is great stuff! Where'd you dig it up?

COOPER: It's a long story . . .

MUSICIAN: I think the boys will get a kick of these . . . (*He goes off.* JACK *appears, carrying an identical stack of musical arrangements. He wears informal clothes: a sweater, gray flannels, white bucks*)

JACK (*as if on telephone*): Coop, I got to talk to you. Can you meet me at Smithers'? (MR. SMITHERS *begins to set up the drugstore counter*)

COOPER: I'll be there. (COOPER *and* JACK *meet at the counter*)

JACK (*tossing* COOPER *the arrangements*): Here's a souvenir for you.

COOPER: What's this?

JACK: Our music. Take it. It's worth over three hundred bucks.

COOPER: Hey, simmer down. What's the matter?

JACK: We're breaking up.

COOPER: You and Kitty?

JACK: Her parents are packing her off to Europe. They won't even let her go back for the second semester. Off she goes, the day after tomorrow.

COOPER: Why?

JACK: Because of that goddam Snow Ball.

COOPER: You were spectacular at the Snow Ball.

JACK: Tell that to her parents. They thought it was vulgar.

COOPER: Vulgar?

JACK: That's what her mother said. Cheap and vulgar. Hollywood stuff. That's what she said.

COOPER: Oh for Chrissake!

JACK: And it didn't help when this *agent* called. From New York.

COOPER: A New York agent!

JACK: He saw us in Boston, and saw us again here, and offered us two hundred and fifty dollars a week each, plus expenses, to work at a nightclub in Toledo!

COOPER: That's a lot of dough!

JACK: And we'd get second billing. We'd go on right after Henny Youngman!

COOPER: Oh hey wow!

JACK: I know. Just think. Dance with Kitty eight times a week, and get *paid* for it!

COOPER: Did Kitty go along with it?

JACK: Sure! She was raring to go! Hell, maybe we would have ended up in the movies!

COOPER: You still could, Jack.

JACK: That's what her folks were scared of. So they lowered the boom. We all had this big scene. Her mother starts to scream, Kitty starts to cry, the old man kicks me out of the house. Then Kitty calls today and says she's off to Europe.

COOPER: I thought her father liked you.

JACK: He did, until the Snow Ball. Now he thinks I'm just an Irishman on the make.

COOPER: Well you are a little, Jack.

JACK: I know I am. But that's not all I am.

COOPER: She'll be back, Jack.

JACK: That's what she says. But it'll be too *late*, Coop! I *know* her! She's lazy. Some guy will give her a big rush, and I won't be there to dance her out of it. (*On the opposite side,* KITTY *comes out in a wedding dress, carrying two glasses of champagne, being congratulated by well-wishers*) So here: take the music. They can play it when you marry Liz.

COOPER (*taking the arrangements*): I'll keep it for you, Jack. You'll be dancing with Kitty again, I swear.

JACK: Oh Coop. Grow up! You're just a dreamer, like everyone else around here! (JACK *goes off as* KITTY *calls to* COOPER *from across the stage. There is dance music in the background*)

KITTY: Cooper! (COOPER *crosses to her*) You haven't kissed the bride yet. (COOPER *gives her a perfunctory kiss*) Oh Cooper, don't be mad. Please. He's a wonderful guy.

COOPER: He's not Jack.

KITTY: He's more my *type*, Cooper. Really. His family knows my family, and he skiis like a dream. We had the most fabulous time in Switzerland.

COOPER: Does he dance?

KITTY (*defiantly*): Yes. Very well. He dances very well.

COOPER: I saw you dance with him out there. He could hardly move.

KITTY: That's because he hurt his ankle.

COOPER: Oh Kitty.

KITTY: He has a bad *ankle*, Cooper. From lacrosse. At Princeton.

COOPER: Bullshit, Kitty. That's bullshit, and you know it.

KITTY: Oh stop, Cooper. Please. Just stop.

COOPER: Jack's here, by the way.

KITTY: I know that. Why wouldn't I know that? I invited him. We've had a long talk. Everything's fine. He's got a scholarship for law school, and made big plans.

COOPER: I notice you wouldn't dance with him.

KITTY: I don't know what you mean.

COOPER: I saw him cut in on you, and you sat right down.

KITTY: I was tired, Cooper.

COOPER: You were scared, Kitty.

KITTY: That's ridiculous.

COOPER: You were scared he'd dance you right out the door!

KITTY (*starting to cry*): Don't, Cooper. Please. I can't stand it.

COOPER (*touching her*): Why'd you do it, Kitty?

KITTY: There's more to life than hanging around nightclubs.

COOPER: That's your mother talking.

KITTY: There's more to life than dancing, then.

COOPER: You were lazy, Kitty. You made a lazy choice. It was just easier to slide downhill.

KITTY: You can't always marry the perfect person, Cooper! No one does!

COOPER: You can try.

KITTY: Anyway, Jack's *found* someone, Cooper! He says he's almost *engaged!* He says she types his papers, and is terribly well organized, and will be a big help in his career. (*The sounds of an airport.* JOAN DALEY *appears. She is neat and well dressed. She looks around impatiently*) She'll be much better for him than I'd ever be! (KITTY *runs off in tears, as a* WAITRESS *sets up a cocktail table.* LUCY *joins* COOPER, *indicates* JOAN)

LUCY: She must be the one. (*They cross to* JOAN)

JOAN: Oh hi. I'm terribly sorry to drag you two all the way out to the airport, but I was between planes, and I thought I'd just give you a jingle. I'm Joan Daley.

COOPER: Hiya.

LUCY: Hello. (*Everyone shakes hands. They settle at the table.* JOAN *gestures imperiously to the* WAITRESS)

JOAN: I just spent the weekend at Andover visiting the boys, and I have to be back for a major fund-raiser in Indianapolis tonight, but I thought I ought to stop by and say hello. (*She briskly removes her gloves*) And, frankly, I thought we should lay our cards on the table. Before this Snow Ball thing gets completely out of hand.

LUCY: Out of hand?

JOAN (*to* WAITRESS): Piña colada, please . . .

LUCY: White wine . . .

COOPER: Light beer. (*The* WAITRESS *goes off angrily*)

JOAN (*pulling a pack of cigarettes out of her purse; looking around*): Do you suppose Jack will lose the election if I sneak one tiny little Menthol Light? I mean, wives have to be so careful in politics . . . (*She offers them to* COOPER *and* LUCY *who shake their heads*) No? How disgustingly healthy. (*She lights up and takes a deep draw*) Well. Tell me. How serious is it? This . . . Snow Ball?

COOPER: Sort of serious.

LUCY: Very serious.

JOAN: You mean you seriously want Jack to *dance?* My Jack? Republican Candidate for Governor Jack Daley? You want him to dance around some room with some old flame?

LUCY: That's what we want.

JOAN: The kids think it's an absolute hoot. We all roared about it when he told us.

COOPER: Jack was a great dancer.

JOAN: So he says. He's out in the garage, every chance he gets, practicing to some tape. I mean, who are we kidding?

LUCY: You're in for a big surprise.

JOAN: Let's be a tad more specific. Will the media be there? Photographers? Television? Any of that?

COOPER: Oh sure. It's a story, after all. Downtown renewal, the hotel fixed up . . .

JOAN: So it will be on TV.

COOPER: Local TV, certainly.

JOAN: *Our* TV, too, I should think. Candidate returns to roots, all that . . .

LUCY: Actually, there's talk of *national* TV. *Entertainment To-night* has made some inquiries.

JOAN: Don't count on it, folks.

LUCY: Well I mean, it's a story, after all. Two old friends come home to dance . . .

JOAN: It's a local story, here and back home.

COOPER: Probably. Yes.

JOAN: Suppose *I* danced with him.

COOPER: I hope you will.

JOAN: No, I mean instead of her.

LUCY: Mrs. Daley . . .

JOAN: Joan.

LUCY: All right, Joan.

JOAN: Actually, we *have* danced a little. We've—we've done the Twist. We were—quite good.

COOPER: Well you can dance the Twist again, if you'd like, Mrs. Daley.

JOAN: Joan.

COOPER: We're hoping, Joan, that Jack will dance the main dance with Kitty.

JOAN: I'm the Main Dance, Mister.

LUCY: Well we know you are, but . . .

JOAN: I'm his WIFE.

LUCY: Oh well . . .

JOAN: He can dance, O.K. He can even do a number, off camera, with this Kitty. But when it comes to magic time, he dances with me.

COOPER: It's just for old times' sake . . .

LUCY: Exactly. It's just a fun thing.

JOAN: Just a fun thing? You tell that to the unemployed steelworkers in Gary watching it on TV. You tell that to the farmers downstate up to their ass in debt. You tell that to me, ME, who shook all those sweaty hands and sat through all those lousy speeches for twenty years. "Just a fun thing!" You think I'm going to sit on the sidelines and watch my husband throw away a chance to be governor, just so he can bounce around with some society broad? No sirree, gang. Sorry. He dances with me, or he doesn't dance at all.

COOPER: Does Jack go along with that?

JOAN: He better. (*She puts on her gloves*) Otherwise I won't come with him. Which will look bad. And I might not be there when he gets back. Which will look worse. Now where the fuck is the ladies room? (*Gets up*)

LUCY: I think it's—

JOAN (*extending her hand*): Thank you very much. What a lovely city. What a lovely airport. What a pleasant way to break up my trip. (*She goes out*)

LUCY (*to* COOPER): Maybe I can still butter her up.

COOPER: I'm amazed she got through security. (LUCY *hurries off after* JOAN)

LUCY: Wait, Mrs. Daley . . . Joan . . . wait . . . (*Meanwhile, on the opposite side of the stage,* BALDWIN HALL, *a tanned, white-haired, elderly man in resort clothes, has come on with a telephone*)

BALDWIN (*on telephone*): Cooper Jones?

COOPER (*as if on the telephone*): Who's this?

BALDWIN: It's Baldwin Hall. Kitty's husband.

COOPER: Ah.

BALDWIN: I wonder if I might talk to you about this Snow Ball business.

COOPER: Shoot.

BALDWIN (*putting on a jacket and tie*): I prefer it to be face to face. My plane gets in at four forty-five.

COOPER: I'll be there. (*A white-jacketed* WAITER *sets up a table and chairs.* COOPER *and* BALDWIN *meet C., and shake hands*) I thought we'd go to the club.

BALDWIN: Any place where it's quiet. (*They cross to the table and order from the* WAITER *as they settle in*) I'll have a gin martini on the rocks with a twist, please.

COOPER: Light beer, Martin.

BALDWIN (*looking around*): Nice club. Did Kitty ever dance here?

COOPER: Every spring. In the courtyard.

BALDWIN: She's a lovely dancer.

COOPER: I'll say.

BALDWIN: Even with an old fool like me. We dance very well together. Every Thursday night we go to the Golf Club down at Ocean Reef, and dance under the stars.

COOPER: Sounds great. (*The* WAITER *brings drinks*)

BALDWIN: Well. Now. This Snow Ball thing. How definite is it?

COOPER: Pretty definite.

BALDWIN: Sometimes these things don't materialize.

COOPER: The invitations are out. The band's all signed up.

BALDWIN: Then the die is cast.

COOPER: I'm afraid it is. Some problem?

BALDWIN (*drinking*): Kitty's not very well. . . . Actually, she's . . . in serious difficulty. She's got. . . . During the operation, they discovered. . . . They say I could lose her. (*He starts to cry*)

COOPER: Oh hey please. Would you like to go somewhere? We have a lounge here. We have a library which is never used . . .

BALDWIN (*shaking his head*): I'm all right. I'm fine now. (*Taps his glass*) I'd like another of these, if I may. (COOPER *signals the waiter*) She refuses to do anything about it until after the party. She's heard you can lose your hair . . .

COOPER: Boy. (*To* WAITER) More of the same for Mr. Hall, Martin. And I might shift to scotch.

BALDWIN: She wants to risk her life, come up here in the dead of winter, dance with some fellow she hasn't seen for thirty years. I can't get over it. I can't make it out. (WAITER *brings more drinks*)

COOPER: Do you want me to find some way to call it off?

BALDWIN: She'd never forgive me.

COOPER: Well then look. All she needs to do is a few steps, really. Just a bow and a spin. Then we'll put her right back on the plane.

BALDWIN: No. She wants to do the whole thing. She took the music you sent her, and found some fella who plays the

piano, and she's been working on her steps ever since.
She's very serious about it.

COOPER: Oh boy.

BALDWIN: This man. Jack Daley. Is he serious, too?

COOPER: I think he is.

BALDWIN: Is he practicing, too?

COOPER: I hear he is.

BALDWIN: Good. Because she wants this to work. It's terribly
important to her. (*Downs his drink, gets up*) And therefore
to me. Now, if you'll return me to the airport . . .

COOPER: Won't you have some dinner?

BALDWIN: No thank you. I can just get back for a late supper
with Kitty.

COOPER: Tell her I hope she feels better.

BALDWIN: I'll tell her nothing at all. She thinks I'm playing golf
in Fort Lauderdale.

COOPER: I'll tell Jack to go easy.

BALDWIN: Sir: we have just had a drink at your club. I assume
everything we discussed was strictly confidential. You may
simply tell him to dance as well as he possibly can. (*He goes
off, as the* WAITER *clears the table. The lights come up on the*

Cotillion Room, now all prepared and decorated for the Snow Ball. LUCY *comes on, carrying some decoration*)

LUCY: Cooper! We just heard on the radio. The storm's worse. The airport has closed down.

COOPER: Oh God.

LUCY: I called the airlines. Jack's plane never took off, and Kitty's stacked up somewhere over Albany.

COOPER: Shit.

LUCY: So what do we do?

COOPER: Do? We do what we always do in times of trouble: we change our clothes. (*He goes off*)

LUCY (*calling after him*): And then we change our LIVES, Cooper Jones! (*No answer.* LUCY *throws up her hands, goes off another way. Music. Lights. Decorations drop into place. Guests enter down the staircase in their evening clothes and overcoats; among them are* SAUL *and* RHODA RADNER)

CALVIN (*brushing off his shoulders*): God! What weather!

MARY: Who cares? Look at this!

RHODA: Let it snow, let it snow, let it snow!

A MAN: Dig the music!

RHODA: It's like walking into the Piazza San Marco when the band strikes up!

SAUL: Rhoda never got over our trip to Venice.

HEATHER: Let's hope those Arthur Murray brush-ups pay off! (*She starts a tentative tango with* BREWSTER)

CALVIN (*to his wife*): What say, Mary? Think we can still cut a rug?

MARY: Go easy, Calvin. I've had a hip replacement.

SAUL: Look at the floor, Rhoda. Notice the workmanship!

RHODA: They should've gotten Johnson's Wax to underwrite this thing. (*Looking at tango dancers*) Ole! (*Older* JACK *enters, in an overcoat. He carries a Valpac bag over his shoulder. He is ruddy faced, gray haired, and looks at least fifty. He watches the dancing for a moment then speaks to a* WAITER)

OLDER JACK: Would you find Mr. Cooper Jones, and tell him I'm here?

WAITER: Who shall I say it is, sir?

OLDER JACK: He'll know. (*The* WAITER *goes off.* JACK *looks around*)

BREWSTER (*to* HEATHER *as they tango*): My grandmother danced on this floor!

HEATHER: We should've brought her! We should've dragged her out of that nursing home!

RHODA (*removing her coat*): Oh but the lights, the music! I feel like Madame Bovary!

SAUL: Just don't act like Madame Bovary! (COOPER *comes out, now in his tuxedo*)

COOPER (*to* JACK): May I help you?

JACK: I certainly hope so.

COOPER (*peering at him*): Jack?

JACK (*holding out his hand*): Hiya, guy.

COOPER: Jack! My God. Jack . . . (*They embrace*) You look . . . great, Jack.

JACK: I look old, Coop. And so do you. (*Indicating the others*) So does everyone. It's been thirty years.

COOPER (*looking at the others*): Right. I never noticed. . . . But hey! How did you get here? Your flight was cancelled.

JACK: I took an earlier one.

COOPER: I would've met you, Jack.

JACK: Naaa. I needed to get my bearings. Things sure have changed, haven't they? Smithers is now a video store.

COOPER: Right. But hey, but you're here! (*Calls toward the dancers*) Hey, gang! Look who's—

JACK (*shushing him*): Hold it. Where is she?

COOPER: Hasn't shown up yet.

JACK: Knew it! She chickened out, didn't she?

COOPER: The STORM, Jack. Remember?

JACK: Oh. Right.

COOPER: Let's hope she's just . . . late.

JACK (*nervously laughing*): Where have we heard that one before? (*The other guests have drifted out*)

COOPER: We never thought we'd get through to you, Jack! All those letters, those telephone calls! But here you are! And you get the V.I.P. treatment, buddy. We're giving you the Executive Suite, free of charge, with a telephone in the john!

JACK: Thanks, but I'll stay with my mother.

COOPER (*carefully*): Your wife isn't with you?

JACK: She . . . couldn't make it.

COOPER: That's too bad.

JACK: Yes. That is. That is too bad. Well. I better get into my monkey suit, huh?

COOPER: Come on. You can still use the suite for that.

(*They go off. Police sirens.* BALDWIN *comes on with* LUCY; *both are in evening clothes*)

BALDWIN: Well we're here. And it's been hell getting here. And I'm not sure why we're here. But we're here.

LUCY: I'm sorry, but I'm hopelessly confused. Where is Kitty?

BALDWIN: Getting dressed, of course. I engaged a room.

LUCY: But what were those sirens? And who were all those policemen?

BALDWIN: It's very simple, really. We had to land in Syracuse, so Kitty insisted on renting a car. And insisted on driving at an unconscionable speed. Naturally she ploughed into a snowbank. The troopers dug us out, and Kitty charmed her way into a police escort right to the front door.

LUCY: The gods are with us!

BALDWIN: Then do you suppose the gods could provide us with a good, stiff drink?

LUCY (*taking his arm*): That you shall have, sir. That you shall have. (*They go off. More music.* LIZ *comes on, in an over-coat. She looks around.* COOPER *comes on*)

COOPER: Well, well. You're early.

LIZ: The kids wanted the car. They dropped me off.

COOPER: Aren't they coming? I reserved them seats in the bleachers.

LIZ: They decided on the movies instead.

COOPER: Son of a BITCH!

LIZ: They said you and I don't show up for the Grateful Dead. Why should they for Jack and Kitty?

COOPER: You should have made them stay.

LIZ: We can't MAKE them do things any more, Cooper. They're too old. And so are we.

COOPER: Let me take your coat. (*He takes off* LIZ's *coat*) Hey! (*She's wearing a lovely green dress*)

LIZ: What's the matter?

COOPER: The green dress from Berger's.

LIZ: They had it on sale.

COOPER: You look good.

LIZ: I don't know . . .

COOPER: You look gorgeous.

LIZ: I must say, getting into these duds gets all the old juices going.

COOPER: What did I tell you? (*He starts dancing with her*)

LIZ (*as they dance*): Smell the perfume?

COOPER: Do I ever. What's it called?

LIZ: Some dumb name. I borrowed it from mother.

COOPER (*stopping dancing*): Liz, before the preliminaries, I want to ask you something important.

LIZ: Ask away.

COOPER: Are you happy?

LIZ: Happy?

COOPER: Here. With me. Tonight.

LIZ: You want me to speak frankly?

COOPER: Yes I do, Liz. I really do.

LIZ: All right then, Cooper. Yes and no.

COOPER: Give me the yes first.

LIZ: O.K. Yes, I like getting gussied up occasionally. I like being with you, dressed or undressed. I even like it when we fight. We keep each other honest, and I like that a lot. So yes, yes, yes, to all of that.

COOPER: And now the no.

LIZ: I don't think you've thought about the morning after.

COOPER: Which means . . . ?

LIZ: Which means that after every party, somebody has to clean up the crap.

COOPER: Watch your language, lady.

LIZ: This is no lady. This is your wife. (LUCY, BALDWIN *and the others come on*)

BALDWIN: There is much to be said for a good drink with good company when you're a poor traveler on a snowy night.

COOPER (*handing champagne around*): Anybody need champagne?

LUCY: Notice the decorations, everyone. We're having the champagne cooled in real snow. (JACK *comes in, now resplendent in tails*)

COOPER: Ah hah! Here he is. Jack, let me introduce you to—

JACK (*arm around* BALDWIN): That's all right. We met in the corridor, didn't we, Baldwin?

BALDWIN: We did indeed. And cemented our friendship in the bar.

LUCY (*low to* COOPER): They seem to get along.

COOPER: They seem to like each other.

BALDWIN (*raising his glass; pointedly*): Ladies and gentlemen, I would like to propose a toast. To Kitty.

JACK: To Kitty.

COOPER: To all of us.

LIZ: To a better world.

LUCY (*low; to* COOPER): To you and me, tomorrow. (COOPER *winces*)

JACK: Still no Kitty?

EVERYONE: She's getting dressed, Jack.

LUCY: For a while we thought we'd lost her.

LIZ: Oh well then you could have gone on in her place.

LUCY: What kind of a fool do you think I am?

LIZ: I've never been quite sure.

LUCY (*grabbing* COOPER *by the arm*): Did you hear that? I'm going to tell her myself!

COOPER: Lucy—(A TV CREW *enters. A* WOMAN REPORTER *speaks into a recorder*)

REPORTER: We are now coming into the Cotillion Room of the old George Washington Hotel, as guests gather to celebrate the homecoming of two special friends . . . (*She finds* JACK, *shoves a microphone in his face*) Mr. Daley: How does it feel to come home and dance with an old flame?

JACK: I think you'd do better to call us young sparks. . . . Is there an ambulance waiting in the wings? (*Laughter from the group*)

REPORTER: As a candidate for governor, are you concerned about the lack of any minority representation at this party?

JACK: Oh these folks are a minority. They just don't know it yet. (*Laughter from crowd*)

COOPER (*low to* JACK): I see you're still light on your feet, Jack.

REPORTER: It's hard to believe you'd remember all your old steps.

JACK: I've got a memory like an elephant. I'll probably dance like one, too. (*More laughter. The crowd moves away for more interviews, as* COOPER *steps forward*)

COOPER (*to audience*): What have I done? says Alec Guinness, as he surveys the bridge on the River Kwai? What in God's name have I done? Why are we here in this tacky old room? Everyone's trying much too hard, and no one's having a good time. Jack is obviously in bad trouble at home, and seems to have been drinking since noon. Poor Kitty is probably crumped out on some couch. And me? What about me? My job is in shambles—I haven't sold anything in weeks. I've had to borrow money, just to buy Christmas presents. And my marriage? Have I messed it up permanently? Is Liz thinking about divorce? Will I end up with Lucy, living on sex and nostalgia? Oh, what have I done, Guinness asks himself, before he throws himself on the plunger and blows the whole damn thing to smithereens! (*A cry of delight from the staircase. Everyone looks toward it in anticipation*) And then Kitty arrived and it all made perfect sense! (*The older* KITTY *enters as she once entered in dancing school. She wears a lovely dress, but like* JACK, *she is now much older*)

KITTY: Ooops! I guess I'm late. (*Applause from the crowd. The television camera moves in, and the television lights come on. She blinks*) What do I do now? Say "cheeze," or what?

BALDWIN (*going to her*): You're home, darling. (*He helps her with her coat, gives her his arm, and walks her downstairs. Squeals and hugs as she greets her old friends. Finally* BALD-WIN *brings her through the crowd to* JACK. *More applause.* JACK *bows to* KITTY, *as if it were the old days*)

KITTY: Oh well, why not? Let's do it from soup to nuts. (*She responds with a deep curtsy. Applause again from the crowd. They kiss*)

JACK: You look great, Kitty.

KITTY: I feel like an old Studebaker, trotted out for an antique show.

JACK: No, no. You look terrific.

KITTY: Thank you, Jack. So do you.

MARY: Come on, you two! Dance!

LUCY: But everyone's not here yet.

BALDWIN: It might be good to get started.

KITTY (*to* JACK): Do you suppose we could sneak out and practice a little? (*The crowd calls out:* "*No! No! Do it now!*") Hey, come on! Give us a break.

JACK: Looks like there isn't time, Kitty. We'll just have to hope for the best.

KITTY: I tried going through it on my own. Some of it came back, some of it didn't.

JACK: Ditto with me. It's hard to dance alone.

KITTY: At least tell the band to go slow. Say we're no spring chickens.

JACK: You're young as a girl.

KITTY: Still. Tell them. (JACK *goes off;* KITTY *glances around*) Cooper Jones, is that you? Where have you been hiding? Crawl from there, you bad boy! You should be ashamed of yourself, putting me on the spot this way.

COOPER (*coming to her*): Oh Kitty, you'll come through with flying colors. (*They hug*)

KITTY: Well, flying or not, get me a glass of water, and all will be forgiven. (BALDWIN *brings her a pill;* COOPER *produces a glass of water.* KITTY *downs the pill quickly, and smiles*)

COOPER: Are you all right?

KITTY: Fine. Never better.

LUCY: Surprise, surprise! (*Out comes the old Snowball sleigh, drawn by two men*) Prance, gentlemen, prance!

EVERYONE: You're supposed to be reindeer!

KITTY: Where'd you find that? In the ruins of Pompeii?

COOPER (*leading* KITTY *to it*): Sit in it, Kitty . . . And Lucy. . . . And Liz, sit beside her.

LIZ: You're not going to get me into that thing!

COOPER: Do it, Liz. Please. Once, without arguing.

LIZ: All right. But under protest. (LIZ *joins* KITTY *and* LUCY *in the sleigh. The TV people focus in. Everyone applauds, then freezes*)

COOPER (*to audience*): Oh my God, you see? You see? This is it! This is what I've wanted all along! Woman, in all her glory! (*Indicating* KITTY) Goddess . . . (*Indicating* LIZ) Wife and mother . . . (*Indicating* LUCY) And finally, Lover! Oh, if I could only have all three forever!

LIZ: Cooper, you're in the way! (*The freeze breaks*)

JACK (*returning*): The orchestra's all set. (*He sees* KITTY *and her court; stands enrapt*) Holy cow.

KITTY: Let's get at it. I think I'm sitting on a nail. (JACK *lifts her out of the sleigh, as before.* LUCY *tells others to remove it, shoos the TV people out of the way.* JACK *and* KITTY *assume their old starting position*) Well then. It's all a question of faith, isn't it? I mean, we'll just have to hold our noses, and jump.

JACK: That's it. (*The crowd backs off, settles into chairs or stands along the wall.* JACK *signals. The orchestra sounds a drumroll*)

KITTY (*holding up her hand*): Hold it. (*The drumroll stops*) I don't know . . . Jack and I have come so far. . . . And all these people have managed to brave the storm. . . . Shouldn't we join hands and pray, or sing the "Star Spangled Banner," or something? (*General laughter. Then the number begins.* JACK *and* KITTY *dance their old Snow Ball number, to the same music, but because they're older now, and out of shape, and out of practice, they make many mistakes. Some of it works beautifully, and the crowd supports them with oh's and ah's and occasional applause. As the dancers continue, the younger* JACK *and* KITTY *join them, swirling and dipping around them, until soon we are seeing the number from several simultaneous perspectives—a complicated, intricate, shifting quartet, sometimes gloriously nostalgic, sometimes precariously out of date. Finally, as the music moves to its conclusion, the younger couple disappears, and the older* JACK *and* KITTY *manage a good enough finish to bring on a round of decent applause. At the end, people cluster around them, congratulating them. Others begin to drift off*)

MARY (*to* HEATHER): How can you leave after seeing something like that? They make me want to dance all night!

HEATHER: I have to get up early tomorrow for a root canal. (*She goes off*)

CALVIN: Well, we've seen it. Now I can die happily.

MARY: Oh Calvin . . .

CALVIN: No, I mean it. I've seen the Parthenon, I've seen the Taj Mahal, I've seen Jack and Kitty. It's all downhill from here.

MARY: Can't we at least take a peek at the Grand Canyon?

(*They go off.* COOPER, LIZ, *and* LUCY *are in the crowd of well-wishers*)

COOPER: Champagne for Jack and Kitty! (*Cheers*)

KITTY: No thank you, Cooper. (*She glances at* BALDWIN) I think it's time I was in bed.

BALDWIN: I agree. (*He slips her another pill which she swallows surreptitiously*)

LUCY: Now you and Baldwin are staying with me, Kitty.

KITTY: We can't, Lucy. We decided to stay right here in this hotel. That way we can be off bright and early.

BALDWIN: The policeman said the airport would be clear tomorrow.

KITTY: Yes, all this snow is supposed just to melt away.

LUCY: But we have a luncheon planned. And a tour of all the old sights.

KITTY: Don't dare, love. I'd probably never leave. (*She starts kissing people goodbye, as* BALDWIN *follows her, shaking hands*) Goodbye, goodbye. . . . Lovely to see you again. . . . Hey, don't everybody stop dancing! Goodbye . . . such fun. . . . Come to Florida. . . . Come see us. . . . Goodbye. (COOPER *and* LUCY *accompany them towards an exit.* KITTY *turns to them*) So long, you two. Thank you for asking me back. (*She kisses* LUCY, *then* COOPER)

COOPER: Kitty, you were great.

KITTY: Well, at least it ties things up, Cooper. I had to do that.

JACK (*agonizingly*): Kitty!

KITTY: Did you think I'd forget you? Come here, you sweet man, so I can say a special goodbye.

JACK: We did O.K., didn't we, Kitty.

KITTY: Well, we tried our damnedest.

JACK: We could try again.

KITTY: Oh Jack . . .

JACK: I mean, just dancing occasionally.

KITTY: Wouldn't that be fun?

JACK: I could visit in Florida. Or you could . . .

KITTY: Oh heavens no, Jack. As Shakespeare says . . . (*She gives him a quick kiss on the cheek*) Enough is enough.

BALDWIN (*taking her arm*): Come on, dear.

KITTY: Goodbye, Jack darling. And thank you.

JACK: Goodbye, Kitty. (KITTY *and* BALDWIN *go. More people also leave*)

COOPER: Champagne, Jack?

JACK (*looking after* KITTY): What? . . . Oh no thanks.

COOPER: Scotch, then? Something. We haven't really caught up.

JACK: Actually, Coop. Now I'm back, I'd better go all the way. The clarinet player is an old pal from Holy Angels. He wants to go out and hoist a few brews.

COOPER: I'll pick you up tomorrow, then. Show you around.

JACK: No thanks, friend. It's breakfast with me dear old Mum, then off to face the music.

COOPER: The campaign?

JACK: No, no. Actually, there won't be a campaign this year, Coop. Marriage troubles. Things are kind of messy.

COOPER: Oh Jack, I'm sorry.

JACK: Naaa. Would've happened anyway. This just brought things to a boil.

COOPER: Then come home, Jack. Work here. Run for office if you want. I'll help. Look, I feel responsible. I stirred this up.

JACK: I'm glad you did, buddy. (*Looks toward where* KITTY *has gone*) It was worth it, even after thirty years. (*Pause*) Well. Onward and upward.

COOPER: So what's next, Jack?

JACK: You know me. I guess I'll land on my feet. (*He does his old dance step from dancing school*)

COOPER: I'm sure you will, Jack.

JACK: So long then, pal. (*They hug, and he goes off.* SAUL *comes in, now in his overcoat*)

SAUL: Rhoda's in the car, Coop. She overdid the champagne.

COOPER: I'm sorry, Saul.

SAUL: But I wanted to say thanks. It reminded me of those dances we saw on our cruise to the South Pacific. I mean, it told some story, even if we didn't know what it was.

COOPER: Thanks, Saul.

SAUL: Call me Monday. We'll talk business.

COOPER: Maybe, Saul. Thanks. (SAUL *goes off. The* TV CREW *is packing up.* LUCY *sits down forlornly at one of the tables.* LIZ *comes up to* COOPER)

LIZ: I'll change for the community shin-dig.

COOPER: I'd better do a little cleaning up.

LIZ (*glancing at* LUCY): Yes. You'd better. (LIZ *goes off.* COOPER *takes off his jacket, crosses to* LUCY. *Others continue to drift off*)

COOPER: The snow's stopping.

LUCY: I know . . . (*Pause*) I didn't tell you this, but I was asked out to Minneapolis for New Year's. (*Looks at him*) Think I should go?

COOPER: I think you should.

LUCY: I think I should, too. (*Getting up*) He's very different, you know. He was born in *Bulgaria,* for God's sake. He sells wall-to-wall carpeting, and wants me to help him in his work. It'll be a whole new thing.

COOPER: Maybe that's good.

LUCY: Maybe it is . . . I wonder what we thought we were doing.

COOPER: Putting a little romance back into the world.

LUCY: Oh is that what it was?

COOPER: I thought they were spectacular!

LUCY (*kissing him on the cheek*): Oh, Cooper! You're more romantic than any of us! (*She goes out. He watches her go. The lights dim on the room. The* REPORTER *and* CAMERAMAN *are puttering with their equipment*)

COOPER: Did you get it, people?

CAMERAMAN: What's to get? Some fat guy pushing an old broad around the room.

COOPER: I don't believe I heard you correctly.

CAMERAMAN: Hey. You get better dancing every day on MTV.

COOPER: You have no idea what you're talking about.

CAMERAMAN: You speaking to me, buddy?

REPORTER: Let's split, Eddie. O.K.?

COOPER (*coming up to the* CAMERAMAN): I'll tell you what you
saw tonight. You saw a class act. You saw a man and a
woman dance beautifully together. You saw the man lead
and the woman follow—no, that's wrong, you saw her
choose to follow, of her own accord. You saw grace and
charm and harmony between the sexes. You saw an image
of civilization up there tonight, that's what you fucking well
saw! (*He shoves him*)

CAMERAMAN: Want to make something of it, buddy?

REPORTER: Forget it, Eddie. He's drunk.

COOPER: Sure I want to make something of it. (*More shoving,
and suddenly both are punching and wrestling on the floor*)

REPORTER: Break it up, fellas! Hey! Break it up! (LIZ *comes on,
now in slacks and parka, sees the fight*)

LIZ: Oh Good Lord! (*She grabs the silver container for the
champagne, and pours it over the wrestlers drenching them
in snow*) The interventionist hereby intervenes! (*They pull
apart, sputtering*)

REPORTER (*helping the* CAMERAMAN *up*): Come on, Eddie. We
can still catch the end of the basketball game.

CAMERAMAN (*as they go*): If you ruined my utility belt, I'll sue
your ass off!

LIZ: Bug off! Or I'll have you arrested under Title Five! (*The TV crew goes.* LIZ *helps* COOPER *up*)

COOPER: What's Title Five?

LIZ: I have no idea. . . . What happened?

COOPER (*putting on his jacket*): I was defending western civilization.

LIZ: Tell me about it in the car. Where's your overcoat?

COOPER: In the check room.

LIZ: Wait here. I'll get it. (*She goes out.* COOPER *looks at the empty Cotillion Room, which is now almost in darkness. The music comes up eerily*)

COOPER (*to audience*): Kitty died in June, holding on longer than anyone expected. Good old Kitty, late at the last. Baldwin brought her back here for burial, and we had a small service down at the club. As for Jack, he made a very gentlemanly speech withdrawing from the election, and left Indiana permanently. We now hear he's running a chain of liquor stores in Phoenix, Arizona, and from all reports, doing reasonably well. (LIZ *comes back on, hands* COOPER *his overcoat*)

LIZ: Put this on before you catch cold.

COOPER: Thanks.

LIZ: Now give me the parking ticket. I'll bring the car around. (*He does; she goes off.* COOPER *puts on his overcoat*)

COOPER (*to audience*): No one ever again tried to revive the Snow Ball. It was over, done with, kaput. But as time went on, it was quite the thing to say you'd been there, at the last one, when Jack Daley danced with Kitty Price for the last time. (*The older* JACK *and* KITTY *dance on*) O.K., O.K., maybe it was just a fat guy pushing an old broad around the room, but the older we got, the more we remembered a stalwart young man and a classy young woman, he proudly deliberate, she deliciously late, dancing together, on into the night. . . . (*Younger* JACK *and* KITTY *take over.* LIZ *comes back on*)

LIZ: O.K. All set with the car.

COOPER: Do we have to go to the Community Center?

LIZ: Nope. Let's go home. The snow's almost stopped, by the way.

COOPER: Hand me the keys. I'll drive.

LIZ: I'd just as soon drive, Cooper.

COOPER: Come on. It'll still be slippery out there.

LIZ: Which is exactly why I should drive . . . (*They go off arguing as the lights fade on the young* JACK *and* KITTY *dancing beautifully in a spot, as they did at the beginning*)

CURTAIN